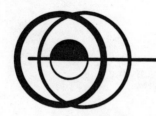

BETTER HEALTH
WITH
SELF-HYPNOSIS

FRANK S. CAPRIO, M.D.

D1227548

Parker Publishing Company
West Nyack, New York

Library of Congress Cataloging in Publication Data

Caprio, Frank Samuel
    Better health with self-hynosis.

    Includes index.
    1. Health 2. Autogenic training. 3. Mind
and body. I. Title.
RA776.5.C36   1985   613   85-3399

ISBN 0-13-071853-X
ISBN 0-13-071846-7 {PBK}

Printed in the United States of America

PREFACE

More and more people are finding "Do-it-yourself" ways of improving themselves. They are seeking better mental and physical health and are desirous of developing a fuller and richer life.

The person who has a sincere and genuine desire to improve his thinking, his health and his way of living can bring this about through his own efforts, provided he is given some guidance—where to begin this overall plan of self-improvement.

Everyone would like to enjoy better health, everyone would like to be happy. Everyone would like to experience the satisfaction of having made a success of his life.

No one can deny that each of us is influenced by our own thoughts. Anyone can master the technique of self-hypnotism. It can lead to a deeper understanding of our inner self.

Self-knowledge inspires self-confidence. In turn, self-confidence leads to successful self-discipline.

One of my teachers, the late Leslie Lecron, clinical psychologist and hypnotist, described his formula for self-improvement as follows:

> Exploring the inner mind is the key to knowing yourself. It will unlock the door to the reasons for character and behavior problems, for emotional disturbances and illnesses, for traits such as phobias and fears and anxiety and many other personal problems such as everyone has. When you know the motivations and reasons behind these things, it is far easier to solve or overcome them and to make the changes that will bring health, happiness and success.

5

It is my sincere hope that those of you who wish to attain self-mastery through self-hypnosis will put into practice what you are about to learn. Your reward will be better physical and mental health, peace of mind, success, and a happier way of life.

Frank S. Caprio, M.D.

Acknowledgments

I wish to express my sincere gratitude to my wife (Louise), author in her own right, for many helpful suggestions and encouragement; to Hal Lynch and David Wright, editors of Prentice-Hall, for their generous assistance with the revision of the final manuscript; to Rosemarie Stevens, Yvonne Varra, Maxine Rose, and Dr. Garland Fross for making available to me material that I incorporated into the manuscript; to those patients who allowed me to include their personal experiences regarding how self-hypnosis enabled them to develop a better-health way of life.

F.S.C.

Also by Frank S. Caprio, M.D.

HELPING YOURSELF WITH
  SELF-HYPNOSIS

HOW TO ENJOY YOURSELF: The
  Antidote Book for Unhappiness and
  Depression

Introduction*

Despite the fact that the American Medical Association recognizes hypnosis as a valuable tool in medicine, many people are still apprehensive about accepting it. Hypnosis is a "state of mind" and is part of everyday life. Unfortunately, people have been misled and influenced by the unethical use of hypnotism employed by stage magicians as entertainment in which they turn audience participants into clucking chickens to evoke laughter.

In the so-called "hypnotic state of mind" one feels very relaxed both physically and mentally and during such a mood inhibitions caused by negative thoughts are weakened or put off guard so that positive life-enhancing, confidence-building, self-improving suggestions can take place, thereby heightening the quality of our life. William James summed it up by saying, "Human beings can alter their lives by altering their attitudes of mind."

Today, many physicians and dentists use hypnosis to help patients promote healing, reduce and control pain, and even control bleeding. In most instances, ethical hypnotists work in conjunction with or on referral by a physician.

The uses of hypnosis are as broad as the spectrum of human needs and problems. Hypnosis and self-hypnosis enable a person to conquer habits detrimental to better health.

Contrary to popular belief, anyone can be hypnotized if he wants to be, if he trusts the hypnotist and if he is not afraid of "losing control." The fact is, there is nothing to be afraid of because hypnotized persons never lose control, are always conscious, and would never do anything against their own wishes.

---

*Excerpts from an article entitled "Are You Hip to Hypnosis" by Maxine Rose, published in *Real Estate Pictorial Magazine* and distributed worldwide.

According to the Florida Association for Professional Hypnosis, hypnosis is no more harmful than sleep.

An article on hypnosis in the January 1980 *Reader's Digest* says that "it is estimated by most experts that 50 to 90 percent of the population can benefit to some degree from hypnosis because the power of the mind is therapeutic." Perhaps that is why people seek out hypnotists for relief from a myriad of ailments; migraine sufferers to lose their headaches, stutterers to express themselves normally, insomniacs to regain their ability to sleep; prospective fliers to overcome the fear of flying, artists to remove frustrating blocks to creativity, and executives leading stress-filled lives to learn how to relax in order to maintain mental and physical health.

Dr. Lorraine Sweeney, of the Seton Medical Center in Chicago, is one of a growing number of pediatricians who use hypnosis to treat children suffering from nail-biting, bed-wetting and other physical problems. She then teaches them *self-hypnosis* so that these children can reinforce the positive suggestions at home and learn to control these afflictions. Dr. Sweeney says that, while much about hypnosis and self-hypnosis is still poorly understood, recent experimental advances have given the practice of hypnosis a new respectability among doctors.

Dr. Carl Simonton, Head of the Cancer Counseling Center in Forth Worth, Texas, calls his miracle method "image therapy." After putting a patient into a hypnotic state, he instructs him to conjure up a mental picture of healthy white blood cells destroying the cancer-ridden cells. His co-workers report he has achieved fantastic success with his "visual imagery" therapy.

Here is what Dr. Simonton has to say, elaborating on the power of *imagery* in healing.

> For years I have believed in the power of visualization (creating the right images of what you desire) and have had reason for doing so because this mental practice has saved my life on a number of occasions, one of them as early as 1920. Today, increasing numbers of the medical

8

profession—doctors, surgeons, and psychiatrists are adding the power of visualization to their treatments, encouraging patients with cancer and other serious illnesses to *picture* their restoration to health in association with various medical aids."

Dr. Simonton goes on:

There is no longer any question that the visualizing power of mind, rightly used, can often help bring about a healing of physical and mental illnesses, whatever they may be. Where a patient's attitude is positive, where he is not willing to die, because he has too many things yet to do, and where he PICTURES himself in a restored sense of health, the *different cells of the body* respond to such *visualization* and he often *gets well.*

Incidentally, if you wish to know more about this "miracle visual imagery" write to Oncology Associations, 1413 Eighth Avenue, Forth Worth, Texas.

In 1922 Emile Coué wrote "With our knowledge of the powerful effect which an idea produces we shall see the importance of exercising a more careful censorship over the thoughts which enter our minds." He recommends that we seek ideas for better health, goodness and success to avoid ailments by unhealthy ideas. This advice is just as sound and true today as it was when Emile Coué first wrote it.

Nevertheless, it is encouraging to realize that hypnosis and self-hypnosis are coming into their own rights in the world of medicine.

CONTENTS

Contents

Contents

Self-hypnosis is a very powerful tool. The effectiveness
of the tool is based upon a person's ability to take re-
sponsibility for himself and his life style; a person's ability to be ready for change.

Through self-hypnosis a person can prevent, re-
store and often cure. He can learn to direct his power,
his energy, his thoughts, and his life, in a very creative
and dynamic way.

Peggy Barrett, R.N. R.H.

CHAPTER 1

PHYSICAL FITNESS: HOW TO LOOK AND FEEL BETTER WITH SELF-HYPNOSIS

MAKE EXERCISE RECREATIONAL

Exercise in moderation is essential to good health. But one must keep in mind that over-exertion can be harmful.

We can't all develop the shoulders of a piano-mover or the biceps of a Hercules. And why in the world should we want to? Swinging dumbbells in a gym class to the point of exhaustion is unintelligent and boring. It may also be dangerous.

An important point is to get fun out of your preferred form of exercise—walking, jogging, dancing, swimming, golf, bowling, bicycling and such. These generally get us out of ruts. They help develop a trim figure and make us feel better.

One great trouble with exercise is that it can quickly become routine. There is little mental refreshment in it. Many a man goes through his "daily dozen" with his mind deeply intent on the cares and perplexities of the day. That isn't exercise; it is merely habit indulgence.

Some men grapple with regimented exercise just as they might tackle a tough and disagreeable business problem. They mechanically go through some set routine with grim resolution to see it through even though it kills them. Sometimes it does.

It would be wiser to consult your doctor as to what form and degree of exercise are best for you, depending on your age and weight.

Don't depend on exercise completely to reduce weight. It merely firms muscles. To reduce, cut your intake of food, particularly carbohydrates. It's just about as simple as that.

Before taking on any exercise program, have a complete physical. Do only exercises prescribed by your physician. Take it easy. Don't do anything beyond your capacity.

How many friends do you know who have allowed themselves to become flabby, neglected their personal appearance, preferred irregular living habits and manifested their loss of pride by developing a lazy disposition? Too many.

Exercise in moderation—the right kind of exercise—improves circulation and physical efficiency by restoring the tonicity of fatigued muscles and maintaining the symmetry of your physique. It has a proper, rational place in your better health program.

MIND RELAXATION WITH MUSCLE STIMULATION

To look well, feel better, you must *think* well. And to think well you must live well. This means safeguarding your health and general well-being.

To repeat, the body needs exercise and your mind needs amusement. You should get some fun out of whatever you do for relaxation. Unenjoyable exercise is the worst kind of exercise for you and is probably doing you more harm than good. Stop it and take up something that interests you—something, if possible, that will combine mind-relaxation with muscle stimulation.

HOLISTIC MEDICINE (BODY-MIND HEALTH)

I encountered an exercise book by Tony Cacciotti subtitled "The Feel Good About Yourself Workout." The book covers an aspect of "Holistic Medicine"—health management and disease prevention through the care of the *whole* person—mind and body.

Cacciotti claims better health refers to wellness, a self-managed program of proper nutrition, balanced exercise, stress management, adequate relaxation and—most important—a commitment to get healthy (physically fit) and to stay that way.

His theory is that *will* is the capacity each individual has to make and carry through decisions about what he or she will and will not allow his or her body to do.

15

Cacciotti believes that a "well-toned body is within the reach of every person, regardless of age, with proper exercises."

No one is more concerned about looking well and feeling good than celebrities who are forever in the spotlight, according to Peter Lupus and Samuel Homola, authors of a *Body-Improvement Guide for Men and Women*.

You don't have to be a celebrity to look like one. We all want to feel better, look better, and live longer with the easiest, most effective methods available to us.

Your body is *you*. Lupus and Homola claim that you can be ugly, weak, and sick or you can be beautiful, strong, and healthy. It's up to you. With a good body you'll be happier and more successful—and you'll feel good about yourself. You'll be filled with energy and self-confidence.

Incidentally, it has been reported that men and women 56 through 87 who were put through a program of walking, swimming, calisthenics and stretching exercises showed a drop in blood pressure, loss of fat, drop in nervous tension and increase in muscle strength.

This is substantiated by a friend of mine—Fred, age 56 and married, who boasts of being in excellent health, which he attributes to exercising via *running* five or six miles three times a week. He informed me that he has been able to lower his blood pressure to normal because of his scheduled thrice-weekly runs. His weight has been consistently normal. He sleeps better, has a healthy appetite and finds running a source of mental as well as physical relaxation.

I had occasion recently to teach Fred self-hypnotism at his request. He uses it in combination with his exercise program to alleviate nervous tension and fatigue which he complained about at one time.

He also plays golf on week-ends which he enjoys. He does not eat "junk-food" and takes vitamins which he feels are essential.

When I asked him why he selected running as his favorite form of exercise he told me he was on the track team during his college years. Since then he has always given the same care to his body as he did during his college days.

I asked Fred "What conclusion have you come to regarding the importance of exercise based on your own experience?"

He replied, "Exercise prolongs your life. . It acts as a tranquilizer. I feel more relaxed physically and mentally after running. It has enabled me to enjoy better health.

"I discovered also that I have been less susceptible to colds, headaches, indigestion, and other symptoms.

"I plan to continue exercising in my later years especially since my doctor, following my semiannual checkups, finds me in excellent health.

"As for self-hypnotism, it has helped me to eliminate needless worrying and is responsible for a feeling of inner contentment."

KEEPING PHYSICALLY FIT IS ANTI-AGING

"Ponce de Leon never found the fabled Fountain Of Youth in the 16th century because there was no such thing," said Michael Briley, author of *Exercise Antidote to Aging,* but there is a second best. Indeed, people in their 60s and 70s can regain much of the vigor they had 20 or so years ago, enabling them to enjoy a fuller, richer life. The secret? No secret at all. The closest thing we have to an anti-aging formula is exercise.

Carol, a widow in her eighties, whom I interviewed informed me she plays 18 holes of golf and enjoys good health. She loves the outdoors, loves to walk and refuses to worry about growing old. Her positive mental attitude (PMA) accounts for her looking good, feeling well, and living longer.

SENIOR OLYMPICS

It was my good fortune to have had the opportunity of interviewing Manya Joyce, Executive Director of Florida Senior Olympics.

She observed that many people retire into mental and

physical stagnation. It has been her intention to spark new vitality in the lives of persons past 50—"It's a pleasure to know that older people do not have to waste time sitting in front of a television set every day—the Senior Olympics program provides a psychological boost for elderly people,—It's a form of reaching out to grab life, and that regenerates the body and mind."

While she realizes that exercise is important she feels that competitive sports are even better—it gives people inspiration and determination to stay physically fit—"We seek to encourage all adults to exercise regularly for better health, happiness and productivity."

Manya Joyce is to be congratulated for bringing to the attention of senior citizens the importance of physical fitness, for staying young, living longer, and enjoying life more. Here is what Burt Reynolds wrote to Manya:

"Physical fitness is extremely important to every age and the Senior Olympics goal of enhancing physical and mental well-being in older adults should attract citizens from all over the nation."

Douglas Fairbanks, Jr. also wrote to Manya:

"Your spirit and vitality are not only to be congratulated, but to be envied. I think it is great that so many of our senior generation are having the opportunity through your program to find enjoyment, as well as better mental and physical health, by participating in these competitive events you are planning."

Now that you have been convinced we all ought to be physically fit, that the physical conditioning of your body is all-important, *self-hypnosis* can add not only years to your life, it can tone up flabby muscles, reduce excessive weight, and improve your overall general health.

Proper exercise—the physical approach to solving your problems can help you attain a healthier and more satisfying life.

Never has there been such a great need for physical fitness as evidenced by the flood of books currently available dealing with the development of a sound body and mind.

Edward O'Relly, an authority on Health Education

wrote: "You need regular, systematic physical exercise to keep every muscle in your body strong, healthy, flexible, and efficient. You need regular planned exercise to keep all your internal organs healthy, and functioning efficiently."

Many men and women who neglect the importance of keeping physically fit are guilty consciously or subconsciously of being too lazy to engage in some form of daily exercise.

Cherry Lowman, who received her Ph.D. in anthropology from Columbia University and has had more than 14 years of professional experience in the social and health research fields, discovered that physical fitness is good *preventive medicine*. She claims also that being fit means more than a longer life—that "it gives us the means for a broader slice of living."

She recommends bicycling, walking, or swimming in your regular weekly fitness program. If you can exercise to music it is even more enjoyable. She points out that fitness gives you an opportunity to try new sports, join new clubs, and make new friends.

If you would like to earn more about enjoying better health through exercise and physical fitness, send for *Revive Fitness Manual*. It tells you how to set up your own exercise program. For your postpaid copy, send $1.50 and a self-addressed envelope to Revive Fitness Manual. Register and Tribune Syndicate, Box 4994, Des Moines, IA 50306

HELPING YOURSELF WITH SELF-HYPNOSIS

To induce the state of self-hypnosis follow these instructions carefully.

Select a room in your home or apartment where you will be assured that you will not be distracted by telephone calls or unnecessary noises. Lie down on a bed or couch or semi-reclining chair, placing your feet on a hassock. Loosen tight clothes. Take three deep breaths. Breathe slowly and deeply. Close your eyes and begin what is known as *Progressive Relaxation*. Repeat each sentence slowly to yourself, letting each command take effect before going on.

I am going to be completely relaxed from my toes to my head. I am going to feel relaxed all over. My feet are relaxed. They feel numb. The feeling of relaxation is traveling from my ankles to my knees. The muscles of my legs are becoming more and more relaxed. I feel the muscles of my thighs, up to my hips, are relaxed. My hips are becoming numb and I feel relaxed in the area of my abdomen progressing upward to my chest muscles. With each breath I get a wonderful feeling of calmness. My neck muscles are relaxing. My face and eyes are relaxing. My mind is relaxing. My entire body is relaxed.

Self-hypnosis works on the theory of suggestibility. Just as we are susceptible to being influenced by others we are susceptible to being influenced by our own thoughts. The voluntary acceptance of a suggestion is essential to successful self-hypnosis.

Through persistent practice you can increase your receptivity to suggestion. A "suggestibility test" is a test to determine your ability to accept and be influenced by a suggestion, thought, or idea either given to you by another person or self-given.

Assuming you have learned to relax yourself physically, the next step is to find out just how suggestible you are.

Test yourself to determine how successful you'll be in achieving the true state of self-hypnotism.

EYE-CLOSURE TEST

Pick a spot on the ceiling. Keep staring at this one spot. Count slowly to ten and see if you can get your eyelids to close at the count of ten. If you experience the irresistible urge to close your eyes on or before the count of ten, you know you are in a state of heightened suggestibility. This is the first test for determining if you have achieved self-hypnotism.

Repeat to yourself:

As I count to ten my eyelids will become very heavy and tired. Even before I complete the count to ten, it may be necessary for me to close my eyes. The moment I do, I shall fall into the self-hypnotic state.

One, my eyelids are becoming very heavy. Two, my eyelids are becoming very tired. Three, I can hardly keep my eyes open.

Continue counting to ten and close your eyes.

So far you have learned the technique of self-relaxation and have tested yourself for suggestibility. You are now ready to give yourself the following suggestions:

* I am going to engage in a program of exercises that I can carry out at home, such as deep-knee bending, stretching of my arms and legs, exercising my neck muscles, abdominal muscles, etc., etc.
* I am going to feel less sluggish and develop more energy as a result of daily exercises.
* I am going to purchase a good book dealing with recommended exercises or borrow a book from the local library.
* I am going to like myself more, especially knowing that I am improving my appearance.
* If I look better, I will feel better.
* Positive thinking results in positive feelings.
* To rouse myself out of the self-hypnotic state, I am going to count slowly to five and give myself the command suggestion—*Awake*. I will instantly open my eyes, feeling wide-awake, relaxed and refreshed.

Note: It isn't necessary to memorize every word of the above suggestions or any of the other so-called post-hypnotic suggestions throughout the book. You can formulate your own suggestions, using your own words if you so desire. Keep in mind that self-hypnosis is a form of re-conditioning your mind. It's positive self-communication while you're in a state of body-mind relaxation. It works if you 1) *accept* what you repeat to yourself, 2) *believe* what you tell your subconscious mind, and 3) *act out* what you plan to put into practice. It entails determination, self-confidence, and self-discipline. Convince yourself that you can accomplish anything within reason you make up your mind to accomplish.

Choose your own time to give yourself self-hypnotic suggestions. It can be early in the morning, shortly after getting out of bed and again before going to bed–whatever works out best for you.

Self-suggestion therapy is based on the premise that self-understanding leads to self-confidence which in turn leads to successful self-discipline and ultimately results in a happier and healthier way of life. Self-hypnosis teaches you how to manage your emotions of life, successfully develop personality-maturity and cultivate a better sense of values.

SUMMING UP

1. Get a physical checkup from your doctor before choosing your particular exercise program,
2. Exercise in moderation is essential to better health,
3. Physical fitness adds years to your life.
4. All hypnosis is self-hypnosis (Self-hypnosis can be defined as positive self-communication during a self-induced state of maximum body-mind relaxation.)
5. Weigh yourself every morning. Keep a progress record.
6. There are many kinds of "psychic healing"— meditation, auto-suggestions, prayer, attitudinal healing, etc.
7. Motivation is important in any weight reduction program.
8. Vitamins are essential to better health
9. Self-hypnotism, together with self-discipline, can help you feel better, look younger, and live longer.

CHAPTER 2

DEVELOPING
HEALTHIER
EATING HABITS

EATING HABITS AND ELIMINATING
EMOTIONAL HANGUPS

There is a definite relationship between eating and emotions. Tension can make you become a compulsive overeater. Through self-hypnosis you can dispel tension. The more you learn to relax, the less tension you will experience, which in turn will help overcome frustration-eating.

A husband, following a quarrel with his wife, may wind up in a gourmet restaurant eating and drinking to excess as an escape from marital unhappiness.

A wife who feels unloved may overcompensate for her love-starvation by feeding her stomach wrong foods and becoming obese.

Many persons who overeat are emotionally frustrated. They suffer from "mental fatness" associated with emotional immaturity.

Sir William Osler, the famous physician, advised everyone over sixty to modify his diet by eating less and less each year.

One of the major causes of mental sluggishness is overeating. According to H.M. Marvin, a former president of the American Heart Association, every pound of excess weight you carry makes it necessary for your heart to pump blood through more than three miles of blood vessels than it would have to serve otherwise.

HAZARDS OF OBESITY

Overeating in some respects can be regarded as a subtle form of suicide. Obese individuals often develop an eat-drink-and-be-merry-for-tomorrow-we die philosophy of life. They become indifferent to health complications.

Incidentally, more women than men become overweight in their later years. It is an established fact that obesity shortens your life span. It is definitely a health hazard. Insurance companies and statisticians report that a person who is overweight and is past middle age is more apt to succumb to premature death from such conditions as coronary thrombosis, diabetes, and arteriosclerosis than a person in the same age group whose weight is average or below average. They also point out that a person with a 20 percent increase in weight over normal and who is 45 years of age has increased his mortality risk to 30 percent higher than normal.

High blood pressure is twice as common in overweight people. Diabetes is four times more prevalent. Overweight persons make poor surgical risks. Deaths from cerebral hemorrhage are twice as common among those who are overweight than among those of normal weight. Yet millions of Americans continue to dig their graves with their teeth, so to speak.

Does heredity play a role in obesity? The consensus is that children imitate the unhealthy eating habits of their parents. Dr. Jean Mayer, Professor of Nutrition at Harvard University, observed that when both parents are overweight, 80 percent of their children also are obese and less than 10 percent of children have an overweight problem when neither parent is obese.

Nevertheless, eating habits can be corrected with self-hypnosis.

No one envies the physique of someone extremely overweight or who has the avoirdupois of a Falstaff. So why not strike a happy medium and live in moderation, avoiding excesses?

All of us have food idiosyncrasies and we all differ in our requirements of food, sleep and rest. The average middle-aged man has a tendency to indulge himself in delicacies and consumes more food than his body can use. Some wives have capitalized on man's weakness in this respect, inspired by the old saw that the way to a man's heart is through his stomach.

Despite the hazardous consequences of obesity, 60 percent of persons in their sixties are overweight. It is estimated that over 40 million Americans are 10 percent overweight and approximately 20 million are at least 20 percent overweight.

DIETING

Did you know that the word "Diet" comes from the Latin "diaeta" meaning "manner of living"?

With advancing years the matter of diet assumes special importance. But it should be sound, sane, and carefully calculated to meet your needs and accomplish the beneficial results that are desired. Such a diet must of necessity be developed and supervised by your doctor. It cannot be arrived at haphazardly.

Don't take up any diet—or for that matter even the simple age-old practice of fasting—without your doctor's sanction. Your body is like a locomotive; it cannot operate without fuel. If you don't feed it, your body will burn itself out. The practice may well do more harm than good. Don't borrow a pet diet from a neighbor, friend, or relative whose condition appears to be parallel with your own. The schedule that worked perfectly for him, may, for one of a dozen reasons, be all wrong for you. Get your doctor's permission first.

We Americans in particular are pathetically eager to believe everything we are told, even inaccurately reported theories that find their way into print concerning food and the mysterious miracles it can perform. Tell us that a certain food will transform us and our imagination is at once intrigued. We must stock the pantry shelves without delay.

Don't infer from the above that diet is of no consequence and that you may as well proceed to eat any and every thing that you fancy in any quantity you please. If you are in good health and of normal weight, neither too heavy nor dangerously thin, the evidence is pretty conclusive that the diet you are following is not too far wrong for you.

MENTAL INDIGESTION

Many a case of supposed indigestion has its foundation in worry and anxiety. A man is scheduled to deliver an important speech. He is on edge. At the banquet board he is served some rich and exotic dish. He eats, suffers indigestion and of course blames the food. Thereafter, whenever he sees this particular concoction he suffers a fear reaction. He worries about it, anticipates and not infrequently encounters trouble. The moral: if you must carry an assortment of worries about with you, park them well outside the dining room.

RULES OF COMMON SENSE

Many of us are content to live up to simple rules of common sense.

- Regularity of meals
- Avoid overeating
- Proper chewing of foods
- Eating plain, wholesome, nourishing food
- Avoid hurried or worried eating.

LOVE AND WEIGHT CONTROL

I have observed that love and weight-reduction go hand in hand. A person in love is less likely to think about food and eating and thus is less likely to have a weight problem.

The excitement of being in love acts as a therapeutic distraction from food.

When you are so wrapped up in trying to please the person you love, you are inclined to forget all about excessive or compulsive eating.

In the same vein, wives and husbands who are happy sexually are less apt to have problems with their weight. The simple truth is that a woman or man who has no one to love loses the incentive to keep a trim figure. When you are in love you are not going to do anything that will turn your lover off—like getting fat. Conversely, an unhappy love affair or problem marriage can send you reeling into an eating binge.

Such binges occur about five times more often in women than men—especially those of college age—and may be more common than most people realize, claims Dr. Richard L. Pyle of the University of Minnesota Hospital.

In a report to the Health Insurance Institute, Pyle found that 6 of 10 college students go on a binge at some time, and in a study of 34 women he discovered that they began their long-term bouts with overeating after a traumatic event, such as separation from someone close to them.

In my own clinical experience I observed that a person who's not in love or is unhappily married will often turn to food, as a substitute for affection—a consolation prize.

Overweight couples are more likely to be sexually frustrated.—"If I'm not going to be happy in love," they conclude, "I might as well enjoy eating the things I really like."—that means sweets and fattening foods.

It is my conclusion that the lack of love in one's life is often behind the habit of overeating.

Put love in your heart, and you'll be less apt to have a weight problem. For love conquers all—even fat.

Loretta, who had a very pretty face, lovely black hair, almost perfect teeth, but was 30 or 40 pounds overweight, sought hypnosis with the hope that she would be able to return to her normal weight. She had tried massages in reducing parlors and reducing pills prescribed by physicians, but invariably gained back the weight she had lost.

Loretta tried to fool herself into believing she wanted to lose weight, but she was cheating in her diet and put the blame on the doctor and the pills.

During one of her sessions of hypnoanalysis she confessed she had been spoiled by her mother who pampered her and kept telling her how beautiful she was. She entered into a marriage with the expectation that her husband would cater to her every whim. She became extravagant, buying more clothes than she needed, and would often humiliate her husband in public. His love waned as he realized that she was spoiled and immature. Losing respect for her, he did not hesitate to let her know that he no longer loved her. Her reaction was to eat to excess and to shower limitless attention on her children, hoping to receive from them the love her husband no longer gave her. She developed a feeling of self-contempt when she looked at herself in the mirror.

When Loretta learned to apply the technique of self-hypnotism she developed insight into the root cause of her weight problem. She unconditioned herself from the traumatic influence of her mother and realized that what she needed was less food and more self-discipline. She eliminated all unhealthy eating, especially sweets, and was rewarded by her husband wit h a new wardrobe. She developed a healthier attitude toward herself, her husband, and her children.

ANALYZE YOUR EATING HABITS

If you want to conquer a weight problem with self-hypnosis ask yourself:

How often do I eat?

What foods do I eat?

How much do I eat?

Am I happy?

Is it emotional hunger?

Do I eat to excess because of frustration?

Am I trying to make food a substitute for something else?

Am I overweight because of marital unhappiness?

To diet successfully make a list of the foods you eat and those you should not eat. Memorize them. Know all you can about calories. Know at the end of each day if you have exceeded your calorie intake.

With self-hypnosis you can recondition your mind through self-given suggestions and develop better eating habits.

Decide in advance what you are going to eat. Weigh yourself daily. Keep your weight-reduction goal constantly in mind. Become weight-conscious. Keep a weekly progress record. See your weight curve come down. Reward yourself, after you have made considerable progress, with a new dress or a new suit in a smaller size. Take pride in your appearance. You'll find that when your friends compliment you on how well you look your ego will be where it should be.

Case-Illustration

This case concerns John—a college professor, age 53, married and father of two daughters.

During several sessions of hypnoanalysis it was revealed that despite being very knowledgeable in his special field, he lacked a positive image of himself. He was never able to talk about his achievements. When his students told him how much they enjoyed his lectures, he never commented. He was self-conscious, self-critical and a perfectionist. John avoided attending social parties on the campus. His wife, on the other hand, was very attractive and an extrovert. She enjoyed attending social functions. It was after he had become a college professor that he began to gain weight. He made food his primary pleasure. He also feared becoming impotent because of his diminished sex drive. He admitted that he derived more pleasure from frequent and excessive eating than from sex relations with his wife.

What John needed was *personality-therapy*. It has been my contention that a person who has an overweight problem needs to uproot the subconscious cause of his compulsive eating. He must learn to understand the origin and psychology of his emotional conflicts. A better understanding of himself is a step in the right direction. It results in a better understanding of his overweight problem, what is referred to as "insight-therapy."

John consulted me at the instigation of his wife. She had heard of a friend who had lost considerable weight through hypnosis.

John decided to contact his physician who discovered he had high blood pressure and was 40 pounds overweight. He recommended that John lose weight and suggested hypnotherapy.

Fortunately, John had the right mental attitude about being hypnotized. He was eager to learn the technique of self-hypnosis. He manifested an enthusiastic determination to lose weight.

He became a very receptive subject, was able to completely relax and induce the self-hypnotic state. John had been told by his doctor that his high blood pressure was one of the complications of his obesity which further motivated his will to lose weight.

In his sessions of self-hynposis, he analyzed his eating habits and was able to condition his mind through auto-relaxation and post-hypnotic suggestions that he was no longer going to eat the wrong foods—that his eating habits could be controlled by self-hypnotic suggestion.

He weighed himself daily, keeping his weight-reducing goal constantly in mind.

He kept a weekly progress record and was pleased to see his weight curve come down. He began to take pride in his appearance, which boosted his self-esteem.

He told himself that he was going to develop new eating habits, sensible ones, and that he was no longer susceptible to temptation.

He decided to give himself a session of self-hypnosis every day before dinner at which time he reinforced the suggestions that he was going to eat less, give up second helpings and would not gain the weight he had lost—that his mind was in command at all times before, during, and after eating. He also altered his personality, became more of an extrovert and enjoyed attending social campus functions.

John realized also that nervous tension was the subconscious cause of his excessive eating. Having learned to relax in his office and at home via self-given suggestions, he noticed that his anxieties and tension subsided. His eating orgies and compulsion to overeat disappeared.

In a letter he informed me that his doctor was pleased not only because of his weight reduction but that his blood pressure had become stabilized. John added that he planned to continue to give himself a 15-minute session of self-hypnosis every day before dinner.

THE HYPNO-DIET:

A DO-IT-YOURSELF PROJECT

I had an opportunity of meeting Jack Heise and discussing with him the subject of his book *The Amazing Hypno-Diet* (New York, Belmont Publications).

He concluded that the only way overweight can be controlled is for the person to develop new eating habits. He informed me that thousands of individuals have been helped to conquer overweight with the aid of hypnosis and self-hypnosis.

He added: "Reports in medical hypnosis journals show almost universal success in assisting overweight persons to not only reach normal weight, but to maintain normal weight after they have reduced."

I agree with my friend Jack wholeheartedly that what the professional has been able to do for his overweight patients we can do for ourselves with the practice of self-hypnosis.

Melvin Powers whom I have known for many years is another who endorses self-hypnotism. In his book, *A Practical Guide to Self-Hypnosis,* he states: "Regardless of the reasons for overweight the use of self-hypnotism is one of the best answers to the problem."

WEIGHT CONTROL

During my membership in the Florida Association for Professional Hypnosis, we circulated among those who attended our lectures and our own respective patients, the following information regarding weight control.

Overweight is one of the more common problems that are dealt with in the field of hypnosis and self-hypnosis. Diet control can be facilitated as tensions are eliminated. The very essence of self-hypnosis is relaxation.

Excessive food intake can result from multiple causes: a substitute for suppressed hostility, love frustrations, occupational reasons, sex problems—in short, any number of reasons ranging from tensions to some sort of gratification—from sexual frustrations to an insecurity dating back to childhood. Stuffing the stomach provides temporary contentment.

The compulsion to overeat cannot be permanently overcome by fad diets. What usually must take place for permanent results is a re-education—a "reprogramming"—of the individual's eating habits. Often, the person can learn to be even more satisfied with less food daily.

Under self-hypnosis, motivation and incentive can be improved by stressing purposes which can vary from person to person: health, beauty, social or business reasons, etc. Suggestion techniques to stress correct eating habits are often utilized and the subject is usually taught to eat only at regular meal times. The habit of eating only proper foods—and in proper quantities—is implanted through self-given suggestions, resulting in better weight control. The urge to overeat can frequently be diminished and there is usually a feeling of being satisfied, which may eliminate the desire to overeat.

Through self-hypnosis you can experience constant reinforcement of proper suggestions. Ultimately, your subconscious mind is reprogrammed and the new eating habits can become permanent.

You'll discover that the use of hypnotic conditioning for weight control can be an extremely gratifying experience.

SELF-HYPNOSIS VERSUS MEDITATION

The dictionary defines meditation as the continuous dwelling of the mind on a thought or idea. You can sit in a comfortable chair in the dark or with the lights on, if you prefer, and concentrate your thoughts on a specific subject. It may consist of reminiscing about something in your past life or something that recently happened or something that has to do with your plans for the future. It is a conscious awareness of anything and everything, in contrast to self-hypnosis which makes use of the subconscious mind.

Meditation doesn't necessarily require placing yourself in a hypnotic state or trance. It entails concentrating seriously on a particular thought and achieving a state of tranquility. Meditation is a mental pacifier. It consoles a troubled soul.

Auto-suggestion, faith cures, prayer, overlap. They are all forms of *psychic healing*. Meditation involves thought control. Self-hypnosis is the technique of applying self-given suggestions for the remedy of a specific problem. It utilizes the power of the subconscious mind in contrast to meditation that deals with conscious awareness.

In self-hypnosis you allow yourself to be influenced by your own thought suggestions. Self-hypnosis is problem-solving.

Meditation is a natural form of auto-relaxation. Self-hypnosis influences your inner self—the way you think about yourself. It is *mind power*.

You can combine the different forms of psychic healing (meditation, auto-suggestion, prayer, "attitudinal healing") with self-hypnosis. Self-improvement is the common denominator. Incidentally, taking a much-needed vacation is a type of self-therapy. Happy-hour relaxation is another kind of psychic relaxation and therapy. Listening to soothing music is also therapeutic. Reading good books is another form of "distraction therapy." It gets your mind off yourself and your problems.

Resort to whatever constructive activity you prefer, to help conquer the frustrations of daily living—and make your life more enjoyable.

WHAT TO TELL YOURSELF AND BELIEVE

The following are some *self-hypnotic suggestions* you can give yourself if you want to develop new, lifelong sensible eating habits.

* I am going to remind myself that obesity will shorten my life span, that it is a serious and unnecessary health hazard.
* Self-relaxation can help me eliminate tension and compulsive overeating.
* Excessive eating is a habit I acquired. I can break this habit by the power of self-suggestion.
* I am going to change my eating habits. I am going to eat less and avoid eating between meals.

Suggest to yourself the following reasons or motivations for wanting to lose weight.

* It will improve my appearance.
* It will prolong my life.
* It will make me feel less sluggish and tired.
* It will make me like myself better and give me greater self-confidence.

HOW IMPORTANT ARE VITAMINS?

Vitamins are complex, dietary essentials that the body is unable to manufacture and must be obtained from outside sources.

Vitamins are necessary for mental and physical well-being. A deficiency of certain vitamins can pave the way toward chronic ill health.

Vitamin deficiency, combined with unhealthy eating habits, can contribute to fatigue, nervousness, insomnia, digestive disorders, depression, and anxiety.

I recommend that you use vitamins with minerals for your nutritional requirements.

Many of us are conditioned to unhealthy eating habits. We eat in fast-food restaurants, overeat and consume unnatural or unhealthy foods. Some of us are "sugarholics."

The natural diet of our grandparents has been abandoned.

We are paying a high price and the price is degenerative disease and premature aging. The chronic and degenerative diseases are now at an all-time high.

Never doubt that self-hypnosis combined with self-discipline can help you develop healthier eating habits. The road back to better health is the road back to nature, natural foods and natural supplements.

Walk every day. It firms up your body tissues and stimulates circulation.

FOOD HEALTH VALUES

Vegetables: Nature locks up the most precious vital nutrients in vegetables. Vegetables may be eaten raw or cooked.

Salads: Cultivate a taste for raw salads. This is going to be a pleasurable and rewarding experience for you. Start now.

Eggs: Eggs are one of nature's best foods, being rich in vitamins, minerals, sulfur, lecithin, and all the essential amino acids (protein). Eggs are considered to have the highest quality of biological protein available to human beings.

Fruits: These are very healthy.

Seafood: You may enjoy almost all seafood, including shrimp, tuna, lobster, and salmon.

Meat: Steak, ground round, or roast beef.

Cheese: Hard brick cheese. Use grated cheese on your salads.

Drinks: Unsweetened fruit juices.

Consult your health food store for your supplementary nutritional health needs.

As you develop healthier eating, weight-control, balance your food needs with adequate vitamins and minerals, exercise and build up your nutritional fortification against illness, and develop right thought patterns, you will begin to reach your full potential of radiant health and happiness. You can accomplish all this with self-hypnosis and self-discipline.

Mastering your eating habits with self-hypnosis will enable you to feel better, look younger, and live longer.

Keep in mind that your potential for better health is greater than you realize.

CHAPTER HIGHLIGHTS

1. Compulsive excessive eating is associated with mental fatness.—the product of emotional immaturity.
2. Obesity due to overeating is a subtle form of suicide.
3. Improper eating habits can be corrected with self-hypnotism.
4. Many cases of indigestion are caused by excess worry and anxiety.
5. Overweight problems, in some instances, have been linked with sexual frustrations.

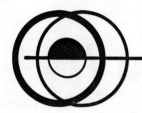

CHAPTER 3

LEARNING TO CONQUER UNHEALTHY LIVING HABITS

HABIT

How shall I a habit break?
As you did that habit make
As you gathered you must lose
As you yielded, now refuse.
Thread by thread the strands we twist
'Till they bind us neck and wrist
Thread by thread the patient hand
Must untwine ere free we stand.

Anon.

HABITS ARE ADDICTIVE

We are all creatures of habit. We have a tendency to put the same shoe on first every morning. We also tend to sit in the same place in the theatre or church.

The majority of our actions can be attributed to habit and as much as 90 percent of our behavior is the result of habit according to William Brown, chairman of the sociology department at the University of Central Florida in Orlando—"Habits are patterns of acting and thinking from feelings of affection and patriotism to the way we hold our fork and tie our shoes."

The development of good habits is part of our instinct of self-preservation. Good habits make survival easier for us.

Habits are created through repetition. The problem is that people are addicted to the wrong things, such as cigarettes, alcohol, drugs, junk foods, sleeping pills, negative emotional reactions, etc.

WORRY

Worry is an unhealthy habit, like any other bad habit. But unlike most other habits, worry can literally kill you by causing physical and mental illness.

You know the saying, "He's worrying himself to death." Well, that's a definite medical fact. I know of people who died because of excessive worry. It's almost a form of suicide.

I'm not saying no one should worry. But it's when you allow yourself to become depressed that worry is serious.

Self-hypnosis enables you to cope with day-to-day living without the constant nagging of worry stress.

Here are a few things to keep in mind—

- Simplify your life. Don't invite complications such as excessive debt. Don't develop champagne tastes on a beer income; that breeds worry.

- Keep telling yourself that worry is an unhealthy habit, that you can control and eliminate it. When you go to bed at night, repeat to yourself, I refuse to worry.

- Talk your worries over with a level-headed friend. It will allow you to share the problem and neutralize it.

- Plan what you want to do and *act* on it. Intelligent action is better than doing nothing and worrying needlessly.

- Be positive. More than half the worry in the world is done by people trying to make a decision before they have sufficient knowledge to do so. Indecision causes excessive worry.

- Be convinced that you have the confidence and the power within you to overcome obstacles and problems.

- Worry is a waste of mental energy. Don't wear yourself out and not solve anything.

- Avoid looking for things to worry about.

- Improve yourself in every way. Self-improvement is effective therapy to diminish worry and unhappiness.

- No one is born with unhealthy habits. They are both acquired and self-curable.

UNHAPPINESS

Happiness is the *absence* of unhappiness. By unhappiness is meant chronic unhappiness—the kind that has become a habit pattern.

You've heard, I'm sure, the saying "He's never happy unless he's unhappy." There is no doubt that there are millions of men and women who are *afraid* to be happy.

Incidentally, I'm not referring to persons who are unhappy because of poverty, a death in the family, or terminal illness, but persons who use situations and disappointments in their life, to rationalize their unhappiness.

You may wonder why people would *choose* to be unhappy. It's because of subconscious self-pity. It is disguised attention-getting, a desire to have the world express sympathetic sorrow for their unhappiness. They make a habit of reminding themselves of past misfortunes. They verbalize their unhappiness by telling all their friends about their troubles. They want to share their unhappiness with anyone who will listen, for unhappiness, like happiness, is *contagious.*

A person who is emotionally disturbed achieves vicarious satisfaction in the importance he creates by enlisting the attention his unhappiness attracts. He wears the expression of a troubled mind.

Unhappy persons have been conditioned to unhappiness in early life. By that I mean unhappy adults, as a rule, were unhappy children and more than likely came from unhappy homes. Continually exposed to the unhappiness of their parents, they became addicted to reacting to unpleasantness in an unhealthy way. They imitated their parents for so many years that they forgot how to react in any other fashion. They became slaves to the habit of being unhappy. They carried over the unhappiness of childhood into their adult lives.

Young persons who suffer from chronic unhappiness should not expect marriage, for instance, to become the solution to their problems. Unhappiness is a *psychological* illness which must be treated prior to the wedding ceremony.

To cure yourself of unhappiness, try to understand the motivation behind your unhappiness. Learn *not* to be unhappy. Misfortunes come to all of us. It isn't what happens to you, but how you *react* to what happens to you.

To remain unhappy is a sickness. Don't be afraid to be happy. Don't use unhappiness as an alibi for not wanting to assume the necessary responsibilities of life. Avoid rationalizing that you have been victimized by bad luck. It's a perfect way of kidding yourself, like winning at solitaire, so to speak, by dealing from the bottom of the deck. It's a lazy way of not working for the things that can bring you happiness.

Many people may not be completely happy, but one thing is certain—they *refuse* to be defeated and they feel duty-bound to live out their lives despite whatever hardships they encounter. They can appreciate the folly of working against oneself—of making themselves unhappy because of guilt associated with past mistakes.

SMOKING

Besides correcting your eating habits for normal weight control, self-hypnosis can also help you give up smoking especially when it begins to prove harmful to your health.

Include in your self-given suggestions the conviction that you are not going to gain weight because you stopped smoking. Evidence shows that many heavy smokers stopped smoking and didn't gain weight.

In your sessions of self-hypnosis, repeat to yourself the benefits of giving up smoking:

* I will no longer suffer from throat irritations.
* I will sleep better.
* I will have whiter teeth.
* I will no longer suffer from "smoker's cough."

* I will enjoy better health.
* I will no longer project "tobacco breath."
* I will be breathing fresh air into my lungs instead of smoke.
* I will be able to save money not buying cigarettes.

Give yourself, also, the added suggestion that you are not going to buy any more cigarettes—that if you should perchance accept a cigarette from someone, you will immediately break it in two as though by compulsion. This will have a tendency to deter you from resuming the smoking habit.

Keep in mind while in the self-hypnotic state that no habit is stronger than the *power of your mind*—the same mind that caused the habit in the first place. It's you versus tobacco. Accept it as a challenge.

Include in your self-hypnosis:

* I am going to experience a feeling of well-being as a result of giving up smoking.
* The conquest of this habit will make it easier for me to conquer other habits harmful to my health.

Suggest away the desire to smoke and the habit will ultimately vanish.

Example:

* I really don't enjoy smoking as much as I used to.

Additional examples of self-hypnotic suggestions;

* I am not going to fool myself into thinking that I can cut down on smoking or smoke in moderation.
* I am never going to permit an exception by smoking an occasional cigarette.
* I am definitely convinced that giving up smoking will add years to my life.
* By practicing the technique of self-relaxation I will never need to become tense and smoke a cigarette as a result.

ALCOHOL TO EXCESS

It is not my intention to persuade you to stop drinking or to encourage you to start drinking. Let's face facts. There are men and women who are "problem drinkers"—who are unable to handle alcoholic beverages successfully. Dipsomania—the craving for drinking is a *sickness* and is *curable* with self-insight, self-education and self-hypnosis.

Individuals who become alcoholics suffer from personality immaturity. They are unable to cope with a major disappointment or tragedy and take refuge in alcohol.

A mature well-adjusted person does not use the stresses of life as an alibi to drive him to drink. Alcoholics are egocentric and unhappy. Unhappy people are more apt to drink to excess. Husbands and wives who are happy and have a successful marriage have no need to drink to excess.

If you have a drinking-problem, you can do much to help yourself via self-therapy and self-discipline. For one thing, you need to analyze and understand yourself. Insight can work as a miracle toward a cure.

Excessive drinking, like chain-smoking, is an *acquired* habit. Since self-hypnosis has proven to be effective for breaking the smoking habit, the same method can help all other habits, particularly those detrimental to your health.

An example of self-hypnotic suggestion to give yourself:

* I have never been able to handle alcohol intelligently. I am going to abstain altogether.

Other examples of suggestions to give yourself:

* I am not going to fool myself by thinking that I can handle an occasional drink or two.
* Each day I abstain is a day closer to permanent abstinence.
* If I can develop the habit, I can also break the habit.

45

* I am not going to use disappointments, financial reverses, poor health, grief, unhappiness as an excuse for my drinking.

Find healthier outlets for the release of tension. Develop an interesting hobby. Read books. Listen to good music. Play golf or some other sport. Keep yourself occupied. Don't drink because you have nothing better to do. Tell yourself also that you can accomplish anything you set your mind to.

SLEEPLESSNESS

If you suffer from sleeplessness you should know something about the causes of sleeplessness or insomnia.

- Taking your troubles to bed. You cannot expect to get a good night's sleep if you lie awake worrying about some problem.
- Being obsessed with the false idea that you just can't sleep. Labeling yourself an "insomniac" merely reinforces a negative suggestion. You begin to believe it.
- Tension-fatigue. Going to bed feeling over-fatigued may cause you to have a sleepless night.
- Bad sleeping conditions. If the room is too cold or too warm, it may interfere with sleep. If a husband snores, his wife may find sleeping difficult.
- Sexual incompatibility in marriage. Wives who are deprived of sexual satisfaction, love, and affection are often restless. They become tense and unhappy. Husbands who are rejected by their wives often complain of an inability to sleep well. Unhappiness in marriage contributes to sleeplessness.
- Going to bed at a different hour each night.

Suggestions (self-hypnotic) to give yourself:

* My eyes are getting very tired—very tired.
* I will close my eyes and sleep will come.
* My body is becoming more and more relaxed.
* I am getting sleepier and sleepier.
* As I count backward very slowly and silently starting with 100, 99, 98, etc., I will become sleepier and sleepier.
* Soon the numbers will disappear and I will fall fast asleep.
* When I awaken in the morning I will feel refreshed and will have had a wonderful night's sleep.
* Now that I have learned to relax my whole body and mind, tension will quickly disappear as I practice the art of self-relaxation and self-hypnosis.

ADDITIONAL RECOMMENDATIONS

1. Use soft music if you find it helps relax you.
2. Look forward to going to bed. Don't worry about not being able to sleep.
3. Think pleasant thoughts. You cannot expect to sleep soundly if you deliberately invite disturbing thoughts.
4. Get into the habit of going to bed at approximately the same hour each night.

HATE

Hate is the very "stuff" of which unhappiness is made. People who hate, hate themselves for hating. The antidote to hate is *love*. It is the most powerful emotion you possess.

Hate is the opposite of love. There are many who do not like to be accused of hating because it causes them to feel guilty. A more acceptable term is *hostility*. It carries a less derogatory connotation.

In the broadest meaning, hostility includes resentments, sadistic humor, unfounded accusations, gossip, intolerance, nagging, argumentativeness and, of course, acts of violence.

It would not be too far-fetched to assume that the ills of civilization can be attributed to a large extent to man's inability to control his impulse to hate.

Some day, wisdom will inspire us to expend the same amount of money, time, and effort toward the scientific study and remedy of hate as we are doing at the present time with cancer, and other challenging diseases.

Why do people hate? Many develop early patterns during childhood.

Children absorb patterns of hate from parents who mistreat them or deprive them of a sufficient quantity of love and affection. Parents who beat their children, encouraged by the rationalization that physical punishment is the only thing that proves effective, are fostering in their children seeds of hostility. Children need to be restrained and disciplined, but never with measures of violence.

Hate is an acquired, *unhealthy*, emotional-reaction habit to anything that threatens our well-being.

No one is born to hate. *We learn to hate. Hate is a habit.*

Fear is common to people who hate. People hate because they are afraid. Fear makes them feel insecure and the greater the insecurity, the greater the tendency to react to threats of any kind with hate.

We can never hope to understand and control hate until we learn to understand and control fear.

People hate because they feel insecure. The person most apt to hate harbors feelings of inferiority. He is frustrated, anxious, suspicious, and fearful. Individuals who hate go through life with clenched fists. They are constantly on the defensive. They are conditioned to hate and in many instances are imitating the hate reactions of their parents.

People hate because they have been deprived of the love they wanted and the love they need. They feel rejected. They harbor the false notion that to survive they must hate. They are encouraged in their convictions by the cynical philosophy that it is a "dog-eat-dog world"—that everyone is selfish and dishonest and that the only way to get ahead is to keep fighting and out-hating their fellow man. For them life becomes a vicious cycle of insecurity leading to hate and resulting in more insecurity. Every day becomes a competitive struggle for survival. Surviving, no matter how, becomes an obsession. They realize the tragedy of their defective reasoning when their cynical philosophy backfires. They unfortunately learn through sad experience that *hate begets hate*, that revenge and vindictiveness are futile.

Fear, for instance, is the end result of epidemics of hate. Even nations are finally awakening to the cold realization that there is no victory in any war.

To repeat, people hate because of fear. They fear death, God, people, and the greatest fear of all—the fear of fear itself.

Hate is an unhealthy *habit emotion* capable of making you sick. Hate induces anger which in turn may lead to a crime of passion. Hate is *habit-forming*. Riots are often incited by hate. When we hate ourselves, we hate others. When others hate us, we in turn hate them. Hating others is followed by subconscious feelings of guilt that lead to self-hatred.

Self-hatred is capable of producing serious health complications. A person who suffers from high blood pressure surely doesn't benefit from feelings of hatred, and spells of anger. Hate is an ulcer-producing emotion. It can cause headaches, and nervous skin rashes, can take away your appetite, keep you awake at night, cause your marriage to suffer, jeopardize your job, and alienate you from your friends. Hate makes you tense. Love makes you relax.

How To De-Hate Yourself With Self-Hypnosis

- Develop normal self-love. Self-love, free of selfishness is a cure-all.
- Don't allow hate to displace love in your heart. Akin to a fire-proof building, you can become hate-proof.
- Don't return abusiveness with abusiveness. Tell yourself that persons who hate are sick. Try to teach the person who hates that it is better to love than to hate.
- When you are moved by the trigger impulse to hate,

give yourself time to study the immediate situation before you say anything or act impulsively. Seek the better handling of what appears to be an acute frustration.

- Don't let another person's hate rub off on you.
- Become immune to people who exhibit an acid disposition toward everything.
- Know that hate is associated with unfounded fear.
- Be kind to yourself. Don't become your own enemy.

When you stop hating yourself and others you have contributed more than your share toward freeing the world of hate. The hate of the world is made up of individuals like you and your neighbor and your neighbor's neighbor. As human beings we are all susceptible to reactions of hate. Therefore, it is our moral obligation to teach ourselves and others that it is better to love than to hate.

Richard was referred to me by his doctor because his stomach ulcer had failed to heal with diet and medication. He hated women and boasted that he was able to force women into submission—that women responded better to men who were forceful and who dominated them with an iron hand. He ridiculed the idea of marriage and cynically stated that love was something manufactured in Hollywood.

Richard had made a career of hating and abusing women. Subjecting them to a master-slave relationship. He enjoyed bullying them into submission. The normal women never went out with him a second time. He only appealed to women who were decidedly neurotic—who sought an outlet for their masochistic tendencies.

A study of his background revealed a long-standing hatred of his mother. Since early childhood he had felt rejected by her. Following his father's death, his mother remarried. His stepfather was an alcoholic. Richard never knew what it was like to be loved by a woman. His bitterness increased with the years. He hated himself, everyone, and everything. His ulcer was the price he paid for his hatred.

I tried to convince Richard while he was in the *hypnotic*

state that one cannot hate others without hating himself. I told him that with so much hostility stored up over the years he couldn't expect to earn the love of any woman, that a man who hates as much as he did was not eligible for marriage.

Self-hypnosis enabled him to dissipate his self-hatred and his hatred of women. He had to agree that his hatred of women was motivated by a subconscious desire to *punish* his mother for having rejected him.

Here are some *anti-hate, self-hypnotic suggestions* to give oneself—

* I have it in me to control my reactions of hatred. I am going to remind myself that life is short and it never pays to become angry over matters that are trivial.
* I will feel good or bad according to the kind of thoughts I choose. I am going to choose *positive* self-encouraging thoughts. I am not going to permit myself to express hatred.
* I may not be responsible for all that happens to me, but I am responsible for my emotional reactions.
* Nothing can bother me if I don't let it bother me.
* I am going to remind myself that as long as I am strong within, free of hate, nothing from without can hurt me.
* I am going to maintain inner serenity and peace of mind that will protect me from becoming a casualty of hate reaction—of hate sickness.

SELFISHNESS

Greed, avarice, materialism, over-aggression, wanting instead of giving, intake and not enough output, and expecting too much from others, all are related to selfishness.

Self-hypnosis can help you become unselfish.

Here are some self-hypnotic suggestions:

* I am not going to exploit my friends.
* I am going to do unto others as I would want them to do unto me.

* I am going to do favors without some selfish motive in mind.
* I am going to remind myself that kindness has its own rewards.
* I am going to go out of my way to do some friend a good deed, even though it may not be appreciated.

JEALOUSY

There are few of us who have not at one time or other experienced *jealousy distress*. Like fear, jealousy is a protective emotion, which we express in a given situation that determines whether or not it is normal or abnormal.

Just as a person may be justified in being afraid under certain circumstances, one can become normally jealous when his suspicions are not the product of his morbid imagination but are based on actual facts.

We are all normally sensitive. In marriage it is impossible to engage in flirtation, even if it seems innocent, without hurting someone.

Some wives, because they feel neglected, think that if they make their husbands jealous, they can rekindle the fire of love between them. Such strategy often results in tragic consequences.

On the other hand, there are men who become jealous whenever their wives or girlfriends dance with the same man, falsely accusing them of being too friendly and question them about every place they go. This kind of jealousy is a hangover from a childhood instinct of over-possessiveness. It is a sign of our own feelings of insecurity and inferiority.

However, in many instances jealousy serves as a protective emotion that keeps the love relationship between two people from getting out of hand. It is the whistle on the tea-kettle that warns us when a love frustration reaches a boiling temperature.

Remind yourself that in love as in everything else you have to play fair.

It is normal for your partner to be jealous when you deliberately break the rules of the game. When two people are intelligently considerate of each other's feelings, there is never a jealousy problem.

FEAR

Fear is another negative emotion that can be a *habit-pattern*. It is influenced by the kind of thinking you do. You can *control* the habit of unreasonable fear with self-hypnosis. Tell yourself:

> * I really have nothing to fear. I have confidence in the power of my own mind. I am going to manifest faith in everything I think and do—faith in the thought that nothing harmful will happen.

Understanding your fear is half the cure. Irrespective of your fear problem, face it, subject it to self-hypnotic analysis and find its solution through the medium of a right mental attitude. If your fears are deep-seated, don't hesitate to seek professional assistance. Fears are *curable*.

Yvonne, a practicing hypnotist related the following:

I was invited to give a three-hour seminar and workshop on Dream Interpretation at a National Convention. After I accepted I began to worry: three hours—what a long time to hold an audience's interest. Even more upsetting was the fact that my audience would consist of my peers.

I prepared a written format to cover the time allotted to me. I included some workshops with audience participation. I read my notes and was pleased with my efforts.

I began experiencing "stage fright." I said to myself, "You teach others how to overcome negative attitudes. Now, practice what you teach." I proceeded to have a little mental chat with myself. I reminded myself that I knew my subject thoroughly and that I truly enjoyed teaching and sharing with others. I further reminded myself that I had been invited to give this particular seminar. They were interested and were coming to hear what I had to teach them. They wanted to learn. They were not coming to see me or judge me personally. They were interested in learning more about Dream Interpretation and I had extensive knowledge of the subject.

I also suggested to myself that I would be calm, relaxed, and confident before and during the presentation. I suggested that I would be well-received for what I had to tell them about dreams. I emerged from self-hypnosis experiencing confidence. I actually looked forward to the convention date.

When that important day came, just before entering the room where I was to speak, I placed myself in self-hypnosis for a few minutes and recharged my positive affirmations. The seminar and workshop proceeded smoothly. I had a truly enjoyable time.

Prior to the seminar I had prepared copious written notes. After only about three minutes into the presentation, I set the notes aside and spoke freely and comfortably. I found myself enjoying eye contact with my audience. I came down from the podium and sat with my peers totally at ease. My memories of that experience are pleasant and I believe my audience found it pleasant and enlightening. I simply gave positive suggestions to my "computer" (subconscious mind) and it did the rest. Since that time I have given other seminars on hypnosis, positive thinking, and other related subjects.

Each time I was calm, confident and comfortable. Self-hypnosis is a marvelous method of self-help. It allows you to communicate with your own subconscious mind. Then, in the appropriate situation and in the appropriate way, self-confidence comes forth automatically to your rescue.

SELF-PITY

Self-pity manifests itself in the form of moodiness, periodic spells of depression, sympathy-seeking, and feelings of unworthiness.

Don't make self-pity an unhealthy *habit.* Use self-hypnotic suggestions, such as:

* I am going to think less about myself and concentrate on keeping myself active in worthwhile projects.
* I am going to avoid becoming a weeping sentimentalist obsessed with feelings of despondency.
* I am going to develop outside interests.
* I am going to develop a positive attitude toward myself and the world around me.

INTOLERANCE

These are a few of the manifestations of intolerance—religious prejudices, class hatred, abusiveness, narrow-mindedness, racial prejudices, snobbishness, unstable emotional reactions.

Calm yourself through the art of *self-hypnotic control.* View these manifestations intelligently. Develop a high T.Q. (tolerance quotient). Remember it takes all kinds of people to make this world which belongs to *all* of us.

Whether you like it or not, you must condition yourself to tolerate the idiosyncrasies and peculiarities of people around you. Avoid rigidity of personality as you would a disease.

Judge a man not by his bank account, race or religion but by the quality of his character.

RULES FOR SELF-IMPROVEMENT

The daily use of self-hypnosis also enables you to formulate your own rules for better living. It is a method of reminding yourself that there is a better way of utilizing your time, a way of planning, a way of getting more done each day. This is so because the process is automatic.

The more you use self-hypnosis, the more you will improve. Your thinking becomes systematized. You begin to acquire a *mature* sense of values.

Start the day with a positive and healthy attitude toward the responsibilities you must face. Organize your time and energy for each day. Work toward making each day a successful and productive day.

The value of self-hypnosis in daily living lies in the fact that it is a technique for self-improvement and successful living. You can use it and attain things you want out of life—more money, better health, prestige, a happier love life, or whatever else you desire.

Self-hypnotism helps you take control of unexpected problems that arise. *Create your own happiness* for it never comes to you of its own accord.

When using self-therapy in daily living remind yourself:

* I need to laugh more for the maintenance of good health, for relaxation of my mind and body. A sense of humor is an antidote to tension and fatigue.
* When something happens during the day and I feel myself getting upset, I will expend my energy in doing something that will divert my mind—some other outlet for my pent-up emotions.

If you experience frequent moods of depression, try to understand them. It will make it easier for you to combat them. The important thing is to do something about them. This is where self-hypnosis can help.

Suggest the following to yourself:

* I am going to stop brooding because I am depressed. I am going to remind myself that depressed spells quite often vanish—they are transient—that everyone at times experiences the blues or low moods.
* I am going to refuse to indulge in feeling sorry for myself
* I am not going to allow myself to become depressed because of guilt about something I can't change. I am going to learn to forgive myself for past mistakes and learn to live in the present—looking forward to a better tomorrow.

SUMMARY OF GUIDELINES FOR HEALTHIER HABIT-THOUGHT PATTERNS

- Accept the hard knocks of life philosophically.
- Learn to control your emotions.
- Try to assume a more mature attitude toward every-day responsibilities.
- Count your blessings and be glad to be alive.
- Never lose your sense of humor by taking things too seriously.
- Make day-to-day living as pleasant as possible instead of painful.
- Develop the ability to relax and enjoy life through self-hypnosis.

CHAPTER **4**

HOW TO ELIMINATE COMMON ACHES AND PAINS

EMOTIONALLY INDUCED AILMENTS

Medicine has made a revolutionary advance in the relief of man's ills. There was a time when only the physical aspects of an illness were considered important in diagnosis. A patient who complained of stomach pains was examined, X-rayed, given medication, a diet, or was recommended for surgery.

However, the science of medicine was not entirely blind to the subjective, the emotional element in illness. As far back as the early Greek physicians, it was recognized that any disturbance of the soul affected the body as well. We accepted the fact that emotions could affect us physically but it was only recently that we realized the extent of that effect.

Psychosomatic medicine today has emerged as a specialty. The very name "psychosomatic" from the Greek words "psyche" meaning "soul" and "soma" referring to the organs of the body recognizes the power and effect of the mind on the body's health and functioning.

All doctors now know that habitual anger often produces stomach ulcers and high blood pressure. Dr. Alvarez of the Mayo Clinic, who has had wide experience in the treatment of various digestive disorders, found an emotional disturbance aggravated the physical illness. Many common aches and pains have been found to be so closely linked with our emotions that in leading medical centers of the country doctors investigate the emotional or psychological factors before making a final diagnosis.

With the recognition that mind and health are interrelated came an even greater discovery. Psychiatrists observed that some of the common causes of psychosomatic illnesses were sex-related.

Proof of the effects of sexual frustration can be found in the records of psychosomatic medicine. The medical profession has observed that many illnesses of the married are due to sexual incompatibility.

Subconscious sex conflicts send women by the thousands to doctors' offices to find relief from some physical symptom.

In discussing the subject of sex and health with leading gynecologists, I learned that many of their patients come to them complaining of a host of aches and pains. They are sometimes reluctant to discuss their intimate sex life, thinking it has no bearing of their ailments. Once the doctor has established the necessary rapport with his patient, she confides in him and begins to relate the details of her sexual dissatisfactions. The sexually frustrated woman is more likely to go to a gynecologist first. When he finds there is no physical basis for her complaints, and suspects that they are caused by a sexual disorder, he refers her to a psychiatrist.

Some individuals go through a lifetime with a deep maladjustment that is not revealed to them until some physical symptoms are severe enough to drive them to a doctor. In many cases psycho-sexual maladjustments have had their real start in childhood and have grown worse during the years.

Bertha complained of an inability to make friends. She claimed that even as a child, she had preferred to keep to herself, rather than mingle with the other children in the neighborhood. As she grew older, her self-consciousness increased. She developed chronic headaches, which were aggravated when she was required to attend some social function.

An analysis of Bertha's background revealed that her maladjustment was precipitated by her parents' divorce, which occurred during her childhood. Her mother was the domineering type and was responsible for enhancing her feelings of inferiority. What all men were interested in was sex. Bertha refused to go out on a date as she feared she would become sexually involved. She became more and more repressed and began to experience tension-headaches. It required re-education combined with self-hypnosis for her to appreciate the relationship between her symptoms and their psycho-sexual background.

Self-hypnosis can benefit you immensely if you suffer from some emotionally induced illness. It disciplines your reaction to sickness and pain. It helps you realize that worry and tension are capable of producing aches and pains and it teaches you to assume a healthier and more relaxed way of thinking.

As I have previously pointed out, self-hypnosis controls the nature of your thinking. It helps you manage your emotions more successfully. You will become a better patient in time of an emergency illness. You will be less fearful in case of an operation and you will assume a more optimistic outlook during your convalescence.

Alice, a married woman, 27 years old, was referred for counseling by her physician. Her psychosomatic ailments consisted of nausea, dizziness, insomnia, and fatigue.

After several sessions she reluctantly confessed that she was unable to enjoy sexual relations with her husband. Her parents had created so great a fear of sex that after marriage she developed an aversion to the act. Her lack of cooperation, fanatic modesty, and fear of childbirth all tended to make her husband extremely unhappy. She boasted of loving Harry, her husband in a "spiritual" way.

With the help of self-hypnosis her attitude toward marital relations was reversed. Her fears disappeared and the readjustment brought happiness to them both, replacing her previous psychosomatic symptoms.

If you are troubled with vague aches and pains that resist medical aid, take inventory of your sex life. Correlate the way you feel physically with the way you are adapting to your sexual needs.

If you are unable to see any connection between a psychosomatic ailment and your emotions consult your doctor to evaluate your complaint.

When a wife is deprived of sexual satisfaction, she may complain of vague aches and pains. If she does not take steps to correct the underlying cause of her trouble, her health complaints become exaggerated.

Guilt plays a tremendous role in psychosomatic ailments.

Exaggerated feelings of guilt in connection with what you do—or even what you think—can make you physically ill. It is not actually what you do sexually, but the self-inflicted guilt about what you do that makes you ill. The sex guilt may be entirely subconscious. You may say: "I don't feel guilty about anything I've done," but the aches and pains that take you to the doctor's office tell a different story.

This is the case of Nancy who suffered from "throbbing headaches." Little did she realize these were the psychosomatic complaints of her sexual dissatisfaction and unhappiness.

This is what Nancy said during one of her sessions of hypnosis:

"I don't want to have sexual relations with my husband. I don't get anything out of it any more—ever since he told me he had relations with another woman. I used to be all right and enjoy sex. But now I have been deliberately holding back probably to punish him. He has his climax but I don't want to be bothered. I used to love him. I get along with him now after a fashion but I have no desire. I find myself refusing to have relations many times. When I do have them it's not pleasurable. I wish that he wouldn't bother me. Sex is repulsive to me now. I don't have any feelings for him. Maybe I shouldn't feel this way. It depresses me. Do you suppose this could be the cause of my headaches?"

Self-hypnosis finally made her realize that she was only defeating herself and that her headaches represented the price she was paying for the revenge motive behind her subconscious "will to displeasure" a term coined by Dr. Wilhelm Stekel. It applies to women who submit to sex relations as a duty knowing that their husband cannot compel them to enjoy the act. This, they rationalize, would give their husband too much pleasure.

There must be millions of men and women who complain of common aches and pains but who are unaware of their association to the subconscious.

The symptoms of a "common cold" for example may be brought on by some subconscious conflict.

The following is Linda's description of how she applied self-hypnosis to uncover the cause of her "nasal congestion" associated with what she referred to as a "bad cold."

"I came down with what apparently was a cold. My doctor confirmed what is commonly spoken of as "catching the bug." My nose was congested. Various medications did little to help. Several weeks went by and I still had a stuffy nose which I felt was a symptom message to me from my subconscious and I should analyze it. I used self-hypnosis during my sessions of auto-hypnosis. I thought of the words "plugged nose." If the cause for the plugged nose was subconscious rather than physical, I would know it. After a few minutes the words "empty"—"full"—"empty" repeated themselves, in my mind, over and over again. I associated the word empty with an inability to have more babies. I felt as if a light bulb had been turned on or curtains parted letting light through. I suddenly knew what the plugged nose-symptom was trying to tell me. I had reached that age in life referred to as the "menopause." Consciously I felt that I had accepted this graciously as I had raised my family and was pursuing and enjoying a career. However, subconsciously it seemed I was trying to hold on to the ability to bear children. I talked to myself at that point and even chuckled as I reminded myself that I most definitely would not relish getting up for middle-of-the-night feedings nor would I look forward to changing diapers again. I further reminded myself that I now had a delightful granddaughter who more than gratified my maternal needs. I then told myself that this was what was meant by the "nose-plugging"—that if this was the case, my nasal congestion would clear up. Believe it or not, my cold cleared up spontaneously.

"Without self-hypnosis and self-analysis as a means of reading my subconscious and enlightening me, who knows how long I would have gone around with my "bad cold?"

COPING WITH PAIN

Today, current magazine articles are reporting the amazing benefits from self-hypnosis, including coping with and alleviating chronic pain via mind control. The utilization of this inner force or power enables you to endure pain with less discomfort. It raises your Pain-Tolerance Quotient (TPQ). One learns to cope with chronic discomfort without being incapacitated.

We all react differently to pain. There are those who are unable to tolerate an average amount of physical or mental pain. Their Pain-Tolerance Quotient is lower than average.

Whether it's a bad tooth, a boil on the neck, headaches, caused by sinusitis, menstrual cramps, labor pains or any other kind of pain, we manifest either the reaction of a child or that of an adult.

The demand for excessive sympathy during illness or suffering is definitely a symptom of emotional immaturity. Every nurse is acquainted with the patient who is continually complaining of discomfort, making unreasonable demands, asking a thousand questions, and insisting on being given a sedative to lessen pain.

The mature well-adjusted individual takes a Spartan attitude toward physical pain. He displays faith in his doctor, is cooperative, doesn't whine about his suffering and patiently waits until the source of his illness is eliminated. The immature person wants to be reassured that no complication will set in, doubts the professional judgment of his physician and displays a "poor little me" attitude as if to say, "Why must I suffer?"

The inability to endure physical inconvenience, whether it is hot or cold weather, hunger pains due to a delayed meal, etc., is common to chronic complainers.

The non-neurotic person expects physical discomforts in life and accepts them philosophically as part of the business of everyday living. Parents are very often responsible for badly conditioning their children to pain and illness.

They are over-solicitous, bestowing upon the sick child too much affection and attention. The result is inevitable. When the child grows up he wants this same amount of sympathy from his doctor, nurses, friends, and the outside world. He is greatly disappointed if he thinks he has in any way been neglected.

Some individuals seem to make the most of their illness as a consequence of the attention they will receive.

There are many men and women today who get very little relief from their psychosomatic aches and pains because they subconsciously wish to suffer, to atone for their feelings of guilt.

Joyce who had been experiencing dizziness, aches and pains confessed that she was responsible for her husband's deserting her some years before. She admitted to having been extremely unhappy, which she claims was the price she had to pay for being unfaithful.

The painful aches and pains served as a way of punishing herself for her past indiscretion.

The need to suffer pain is responsible for many persons being unable to experience a feeling of well-being. They are in constant tension, afraid to relax, seldom allow themselves to smile, and spend much of their time regretting past indiscretions.

Pain can be controlled by means of self-given hypnotic suggestions. If your pain is psychological in origin, correct the cause of your mental anguish.

Learn to control fear thoughts with mind power.

A word of caution: let your doctor first evaluate the cause of your aches and pains before using self-hypnosis.

Norman Cousins, best-seller author of *An Anatomy Of An Illness*, attributes his recovery from a rare illness to his positive emotional fortitude. He points out how *fear* and *panic* invariably make symptoms worse, substantiating the premise of self-hypnosis that a *positive mental attitude* in many instances is therapeutic and often expedites the convalescence from a serious illness.

DENTAL ANXIETY

According to Jane Brody, reporter for *The New York Times*, "For some 50 million Americans going to the dentist is akin to a nightmare." She adds: "An estimated 12 million of them are so panicked by the thought that they never go at all. Even when forced by pain to make an appointment, they are likely to cancel at the last minute or bolt when they reach the door."

Because of this widespread fear of the dentist, Mount Sinai Medical Center in New York City has a Dental Anxiety Clinic where anxiety-reducing techniques are taught to students and dentists.

How does one explain the fear of dental pain?

Fear is a *habit*. Think back to the last time you visited your dentist. Quite likely you became anxious and uncomfortable before any treatment was initiated. Deep inside many of us remember, subconsciously, the old-fashioned bone-rattling motor driven drill that seemed to shake one's brain as it ground away at our teeth. The horrifying discomfort these old drills produced was so unique that they almost defied description.

However, these old-fashioned tooth grinders were replaced long ago by high-speed, water-cooled drills which produce little if any discomfort. Why is a visit to the dental office still frightening to so many people? The memory of the old-fashioned drill is buried deep in the subconscious, the storehouse of memories. Consciously, a person is aware of the quiet, modern drill today, but subconsciously remembers the old-fashioned drill and the resulting discomfort.

Many of today's children have no fear of the dental office for they were never exposed to the discomfort we experienced as children. Could it be that our anxiety is simply a bad habit?

Back in the twenties and thirties, the child's first visit to the dentist was made because the child suffered from a toothache and badly swollen jaw. No matter how kind and skillful the dentist was, the treatment was painful. The memory of this pain was filed in the subconscious.

We have considered a few of the causes for the fear of dentistry. Now let us consider possible treatment or cure for this fear. I believe *hypnosis* is by far the best treatment for overcoming and treating fear. Hypnosis is a state of attentive responsible concentration in which there is a heightened degree of suggestibility. With *self-hypnosis,* the conscious mind can be by-passed and suggestibility can be implanted into the subconscious where the negative suggestions are buried.

The ideal cure would be for all dentists to be skilled hypnotists who use hypnosis routinely. They need not call it hypnosis, if there should be any objection to the terms. One of the best dental hypnotists in Florida claims he "relaxes" his patients.

According to the latest poll, only about 3 percent of dentists in the United States use hypnosis in their practice. This seems strange since as long ago as 1958 the American Medical Association gave its approval of the use of hypnosis and recommended that it be taught in medical and dental schools.

Since this is the case, we must find other methods for alleviating the fear of dentistry.

One alternative method would be for the fearful patient to have his fears removed by an ethical hypnotist and to learn *self-hypnosis* from him. Self-hypnosis can eliminate fear while in the dental office. Thus, as a relaxed patient, your visit will be pleasant instead of traumatic and the dentist can do far better work for a relaxed patient than he can for a frightened, emotional one.

The fearful patient can *learn* self-hypnosis. This may be a little time-consuming because of the common misconception about hypnosis. But it can be learned.

An example of a good learning technique is this:

Give yourself suggestions during the dental visit similar to these:

> I am imagining that I am in a very pleasant environment. I am looking out over a beautiful valley, or a deep blue lake, or a favorite childhood spot.

After you have given yourself the suggestion of being in a favorite spot, make yourself completely comfortable—making your mind as nearly blank as possible.

If you have trouble becoming completely relaxed, this simple exercise will help deepen the relaxation. Make a fist of whichever hand you prefer, with the index finger extended. Preferably moving your lips, silently say to yourself—

> At the count of three my finger will be so stiff that I cannot bend it. No matter how hard I try. I cannot bend my finger. One—my finger is becoming stiff. Two, it is becoming more and more stiff. Three, it is so stiff that I cannot bend it. No matter how hard I try. I cannot bend it.
>
> Next tell yourself—Now, at the count of three, my finger will bend, my eyes will close, and I shall be in deep hypnosis. With each breath, I shall go deeper and deeper into hypnosis. One, my finger is less stiff. Two, my finger is less and less stiff. Three, my finger bends, my hand drops comfortably. My eyes close and I am in deep hypnosis. With each breath I take, I go deeper into hypnosis.
>
> Next, while in this comfortable and relaxed state of hypnosis, silently count backward from fifty to one, synchronizing the counting with your breathing. Each time you inhale, count. At the same time, your suggestion is going through your mind in a semi-automatic way. If you are going through this exercise solely for relaxation or as a learning experience, at the count of one, you will blink your eyes and awaken feeling wonderful in every way. If you are in the dental chair, at the count of one you will continue in this relaxed state until the dentist awakens you, with a prearranged signal, such as touching your shoulder. If you are using this hypnosis exercise at night, after you are in bed, at the count of

one, you will drift into a natural sleep, instead of blinking and awakening.

After the first 20 times of using this self-hypnosis exercise, the counting from 50 to 1 is optional. By that time your subconscious will automatically cause you to blink your eyes and awaken from hypnosis, unless you are in the dental chair and then you will await the signal for awakening. It is absolutely necessary that you and the dentist agree on a signal from you to begin the dental procedure (after you have put yourself in self-hypnosis) and a signal from him for you to awaken at the completion of the dental procedure.

The following is a personal account of how I used self-hypnosis to help me survive a heart condition diagnosed as "Congestive Heart Failure" which can sometimes prove fatal.

Early in December I was admitted to a local hospital. I had just returned from a trip North, having visited my son. When I returned to Florida I was completely exhausted. My ankles were swollen, I was unable to urinate because of a prostate condition, I also developed congestion in my lungs and experienced pains around my heart.

My doctor congratulated me for having the wisdom of calling him in time and I was immediately hospitalized. A consulting cardiologist was convinced that I was suffering from a "Heart Failure" syndrome. I was put through the gamut of X-rays, an electrocardiogram, prostate examination, and various laboratory tests.

Incidentally, the last time I was ill was about 25 years ago, at which time I had a coronary heart attack. It was recommended that I give up smoking. Having studied hypnosis, I was able to hypnotize myself into breaking a smoking habit of many years' duration. It proved successful for I haven't smoked since. I am confident I will never return to smoking.

A heart specialist informed me that if someone survives a coronary heart attack there is always the possibility of a subsequent attack that might prove fatal. He cautioned me to "take it easy" and not overtax myself. I decided I would slow down, but at the same time I wasn't going to live in fear the rest of my life.

With the help of PMA (positive mental attitude) via periodic self-hypnosis I managed to survive for which I am grateful.

It was only natural that when I reached a point of near-collapse, I became frightened. I concluded—this is it—my time is up. I began to have doubts about my ultimate recovery, even though I was in good hands. My doctor had an excellent reputation and I was in one of the best hospitals in the country.

Despite the assurance I received from those attending me, I became preoccupied with a fear of dying. It was one time I realized it was more of a disadvantage to be a "physician-patient." For example, I worried that they would have to operate and do a "prostatectomy" because of urinary difficulties. I also imagined that since I had so much chest discomfort what I was really suffering from was "cancer of the prostate" and it had spread to my lungs via metastasis, complicated by shortness of breath, a definite sign of heart failure.

Mentally I was a mess, perhaps in need of a psychiatrist. I wanted to live long enough to write three or more books that I had planned. Physicians have a notorious reputation for being difficult hospital patients. They worry and imagine the worst. It accounts for the cliché we hear so many times "A little learning is a dangerous thing."

I realized more than ever I had to overcome my pessimistic outlook and stop worrying. I found comfort in the lines of a favorite poem of mine by James Allen:

> Mind is the master power that molds and makes
> And man is mind and evermore he takes
> The tool of thought and shaping what he wills
> Brings forth a thousand joys, a thousand ills.
> He thinks in secret and it comes to pass
> Environment is but his looking glass."

I convinced myself that my convalescence would depend upon the nature of my thinking. I had to take command of my thoughts, inspired by an inner "will to live." As a psychiatrist, I knew fear originates in the mind. Consequently I told myself—What The Mind Causes The Mind Can Cure.

I gave myself positive self-hypnotic suggestions morning, noon, and night, knowing that self-hypnosis is a form of psychic healing accompanied through the voluntary acceptance and application of one's own positive suggestions.

I kept repeating silently and secretly to myself,

> I have the power within me to control and influence my mind at will—I can quickly convert negative thinking into positive thinking. I am improving every day in every way. I will soon be well again.

Then one day the doctor took my blood pressure again and was surprised that it had dropped from a high of 185 to a normal 128 over 80 (it has remained normal ever since). He couldn't get over the sudden change in my overall condition. I had become cheerful and optimistic and began to improve rapidly. I was to remain in the hospital a minimum of two to three weeks. Instead I was discharged after eight days.

By the way, the day I was admitted I was immediately placed in a wheel chair. As I was being wheeled down a long corridor to my room, I noticed a plaque along side the door of each empty room with the inscription "In Memory Of." I turned to the hospital attendant who was pushing the wheel chair and asked: "Has there ever been anybody who recovered on this particular floor?" He laughed and thought it was very funny. The director of the hospital heard about it, came to my room to tell me that with such a sense of humor I was bound to recover from whatever I was suffering from.

I informed him that I had acquired my sense of humor from my mother, who, by the way also had a heart attack around the same age I had my initial attack. I am sure that because of her positive mental attitude, her strong will to survive, she lived to the age of 82.

Her doctor had given her only one year. She lived an additional 30 years. I was away at the time she died but I learned from my sister that up to a few minutes before she expired, she had been up and about joking and laughing with a cousin who had visited her.

I mention this only to prove a point—that it was her optimistic mental attitude in addition to her sense of humor that enabled her to disappoint the Grim Reaper so many times.

Although I may have inherited a family predisposition to heart trouble, I was fortunate to have been influenced by her zest for life, her fearlessness and determination to survive.

I am convinced more than ever, because of personal experience, that *Mind Power* plays an important role during a health crisis. I found myself at the crossroads, but must have chosen the right road. My convalescence was favorably influenced by faith in my doctor, and of course, faith in the Sky-Chief (a term used by one of my friends when he visited me at the hospital).

I attribute my survival to self-hypnosis—a mind-transplant insofar as I replaced sick thinking with positive thinking, resulting in a new lease on life.

I recall telling myself that I was going to smile at my doctor, the nurses, and friends who visited me, instead of displaying a fear-of-death look on my face. When people asked me how I felt, I assured them I was feeling better every day. I kept myself busy reading inspirational books and articles, keeping my mind constructively occupied.

Through self-hypnosis I proved the futility of worrying about complications that may never happen. I was determined that I was going to become a worry-free-physician-patient. I was no longer preoccupied with the fear of dying.

Self-hypnosis is not a cure-all, but I am convinced, because of my own unique experience, that mind-power, thought-control self-hypnosis, call it what you will, in time of illness can sometimes make the difference between surviving and not surviving.

As Herbert Spencer, the philosopher said: "It is the mind that maketh good or ill."

LAUGHTER FOR BETTER HEALTH

Laughter is psychological medicine. It is essential to well-balanced living. Laughter is healthy. It does what tranquilizers cannot do for you—it heals the ills of the soul.

According to the Institute for Advancement of Human Behavior,—"Throughout history, comedians have given us the gift of laughter. In good times and in bad, laughter has served as a 'natural' healer providing us with a sense of well-being and good health we all need."

We are living in an age of anxiety—an era in which men and women from every station of life suffer from emotional conflicts that mar their happiness, undermine their physical and mental health, warp their marriages, and destroy their social effectiveness and value to society as well as to themselves.

I have always maintained that a sense of humor is as essential to normal living as oxygen is to lungs. It is relaxing and acts as an antidote for day-to-day frustrations. It lifts the emotional stress in which we hold ourselves and thrusts aside gloomy thoughts.

Doctors are beginning to appreciate the wonderful benefits of laughter. They have discovered the influence it has on their patients' convalescence from various psychosomatic illness.

Dr. William Fry of Stanford University Medical School psychiatric department informs us "Humor stirs the inside and gets the endocrine system going, which can be quite beneficial in alleviating disease."

Laughter helps to keep us well. It is anti-stress, anti-worry, and anti-aging. It pulls up those saggy facial muscles and saddened eyes to a refreshing smile.

A healthy portion of laughter can be blended with the daily grind and make it less tedious. It enables us to endure the stress-producing realities of life.

"Laugh and the world laughs with you," is an old cliché, but it is good advice. Learn to laugh at yourself and the many funny things about life and the world, and you're bound to be a happier person. There is humor all around you every day. Learn to recognize it and share it with others.

Humor is part and parcel of what makes life worth living. It is a magic elixir that will enrich your life in many ways. To laugh more is to have lived a fuller and more enjoyable life.

After 40 years of giving talks on a variety of subjects to different audiences, including television and radio appearances, I have discovered that almost everyone appreciates humor as evidenced by a smile or chuckle or outright laughter. An audience likes to learn but it also likes to be entertained. At least that has been my experience. I have made it a point to incorporate into every lecture something that will make people laugh—a humorous anecdote—or a joke I felt was right for the subject of my talk.

All of us need to laugh more to counter-balance the anxieties of a troubled world.

We should feel indebted to comedians like Bob Hope, George Burns, Milton Berle, Joan Rivers, and others too many to mention, for helping us to survive the stresses of daily living. Laughter gives us the courage to meet and master the problems of a world in crisis.

Here is how you can utilize self-hypnosis or autosuggestion to acquire a sense of humor. I believe anyone can develop a sense of humor.

Tell yourself:

* I am going to convince myself that humor is necessary to happier living as food is for survival.
* I need to laugh for the maintenance of good health—for relaxation of my mind and body.
* I am going to remind myself not to take either myself or my troubles too seriously.
* Laughter can make life more endurable.
* I am capable of cultivating a sense of humor by simply repeating each day that I will find something to laugh about.

* I am going to interest myself in my friends more and share laughter with them.
* I am going to remind myself that life is to be enjoyed.
* Self-happiness is an attitude that I can cultivate.
* I am no longer going to live in the past, afraid to relax, seldom allowing myself to smile or laugh.
* I am going to put laughter into my life. Laughter is self-therapy. It will make day to day living more pleasurable.

SUMMARY

1. Worry and tension are capable of producing physical aches and pains.
2. Self-hypnotism can influence your reaction to sickness and discomforts.
3. Dental pain can be controlled by self-hypnotic suggestions.
4. Fear of dental anxiety is self-curable.
5. Mind power plays an important role during convalescence from a serious illness.
6. Laughter is psychological medicine. It is anti-stress and anti-aging.
7. A sense of humor is as essential to normal living as oxygen is to lungs.

CHAPTER 5

ACQUIRING A POSITIVE SELF-IMAGE: THE FOUNDATION OF SELF-HAPPINESS

Your future depends on how you think about yourself. You cannot expect to do wonderful things in life unless you first succeed in liking yourself. A positive self-image is essential to success and happiness.

Many of us are unaware of our ability to succeed and to be genuinely happy. We possess greater mind potential than we realize. We can survive adversities if we think we can. Self-confidence is not something inherited. It comes from the satisfaction of repeated self-created accomplishments.

Repeat to yourself:

As I think so shall I feel. The nature of my thoughts constitutes the key to developing a positive self-image.

Losers feel miserable only because they *think negatively*— miserable thoughts instead of positive thoughts.

To be a winner according to W. Clement Stone—You must *think* and *act* like a *winner*.

MIND CONTROL

There is nothing more exhilarating and life-enhancing than being in control of your own mind–of your own emotions and thinking—of being able to develop a positive self-image.

A positive self-image is a pearl of great value. Without it you go through life aimlessly, without direction or purpose.

WINNER OR LOSER: THE OPTION IS YOURS

With self-hypnosis there is no excuse for being a loser. You need only develop self-confidence and practice self-communication.

Tell yourself:

Anything I can *conceive* I can *achieve*. This kind of verbal auto-suggestion can help you acquire a positive image of yourself.

A negative self-image is self-destructive. It can sometimes prove fatal.

Alan Ladd became a loser by choice. Although he established himself as one of the screen's finest actors, he never acquired a belief in himself. He focused on what was wrong with him (self-dislike) instead of what was right and convinced himself he had nothing to live for.

This lack of a positive self-image, this lack of a will to survive, accounted for many other celebrities who became casualties of their own self-destructive thinking and way of life.

Had they had the advantage of self-hypnosis, they could have disciplined their negative thinking. To survive, reason must rule.

BELIEVE IN YOURSELF

Adversity can be a blessing in disguise. Failures, disappointments can become steppingstones to success.

A high school teacher who had flunked me in English once told me that I would never amount to much because I was "lazy." He did me a favor; I was determined to prove he was wrong. I went through medical school and became the author of 33 books.

In my research, I learned about some of the failures of famous people who ultimately became great successes. Winston Churchill, for example, failed his entrance examinations to a military academy.

Publishing companies rejected Walt Disney's cartoon samples and informed him that he had no talent.

The bottom line is to believe in yourself—your capabilities—to hold on to a positive image of yourself and your potentials.

MIND POWER

Your mind has unlimited self-healing powers—capable of not only overcoming habits detrimental to your physical and mental well-being, but of surmounting many of the obstacles that stand in the way of success and happiness.

Just as negative thinking can make you fail, positive thinking can make you succeed.

Convince yourself with techniques of self-hypnotism that you have the ability to succeed—that you can learn to be as happy as you want to be.

If you have allowed your mind to develop the habit of negative thinking, you can use this same mind to develop the habit of positive thinking. Negativism will only block you from positive action.

A positive mental attitude is indispensable to success. Believe in your potential. Don't give up so easily. The things that are most worthwhile are often the hardest to achieve.

With perseverance and determination to get ahead, nothing in the world can hold you back. *Think* success and you will become successful.

Dr. Perry A. Patrick, author of "Hypnotherapy" (*Lifestyle Guide*, Orange, California) claims the ability to make use of self-hypnosis effectively lies within each of us.

Here is his message—"To control our own lives more effectively and manage the stress that comes with living in our society is a dream for millions, a reality for few.

"We all know that it is possible to achieve most of what we desire from life, but we don't know where to look for the solutions to our problems.

"The unraveling of our problems, stresses, failures, and misgivings lies within each and every one of us. Once we learn to use the virtually untapped ability of our subconscious mind, we can walk 'in balance.' However we must make the decision to learn how and then follow through with it."

The following is what Eleanor described regarding how she benefited from self-hypnosis.

Self-hypnosis has worked a miracle for me. As you well know my problem was lack of motivation—just gliding through life, but feeling unfulfilled.

Your 'Think–Plan–Act' formula has inspired me. I include it in my self-hypnosis sessions every morning before getting out of bed. You have helped me to practice control of my drinking and you are helping to motivate me to write. I want you to know that if I'm talented enough and God is willing, when my first book is written I will dedicate it to you—small thanks for all your help.

I also want to thank you for the help you have given my daughter with hypnosis. She has not had drugs of any kind for almost three years. She is enjoying better health and is a happier person.

My wish is that more people would overcome their fear of being hypnotized. I have told my many friends how much I benefited from hypnosis but they still fear it, which of course is due to their ignorance of the subject. I hope that in the book you are writing presently, *Better Health With Self-Hypnosis,* you assure people that there is nothing to fear about hypnosis—that it consists of body-mind relaxation and giving yourself positive suggestions. It's a form of self-therapy and it works.

Linda, turned to sex for acceptance at the age of 12. She had been rejected by her mother, her teachers and even her playmates as being dumb. She left school at 16 and got married for the first of three times.

I subjected her to hypnoanalysis hoping to find a clue to her "reading difficulty" which began in childhood.

I explained to Linda that all hypnosis is actually *self-hypnosis*—that she was going to relax her body and mind and that she would relive her childhood while in a state of hypnosis. This procedure is called hypnoanalysis.

She began by describing her relationship to her mother—"She always had time for other people but not for me. I didn't feel loved by my mother, but I felt I was loved by my father."

She went on "If she didn't want me, why did she have me? She showered more love and attention on her dog than she did on me. I don't hate dogs today, but I don't want any around my home."

It was quite obvious that her hatred of her mother was based on her rejection as a child.

"Once when my mother was in a hospital because the doctor thought she had cancer, she reached out for me only because she knew I would be there."

Recalling her childhood, she remembered how bitter she felt toward her sister who read comic books without any difficulty.

Linda referred to one of her teachers as a "witch." "She told me I was stupid because I couldn't read."

She went on with her unpleasant reminiscences:

"The other children made fun of me. They would laugh and do things that kids do. I just hated that. I might have cried when I was by myself, but I felt very bad. It really bothered me.' '

She told about a special program at school in which the teacher refused to let her take part.

"I couldn't do what I was supposed to and she was punishing me for it.' '

She recalls also her problems with the dictionary, and her teacher's sing-song instructions. "Look up the word. If you cannot pronounce the word, look it up in the dictionary."

"Well, my God, it was just a blank. The pages were gibberish to me."

Linda's mother would get her up at 5:30 each morning to work on reading with her. It didn't work.

I asked Linda, "Is it possible the rejection by your mother caused you to punish her—to get even?"

"It wouldn't have been worth the price I had to pay for it," Linda answered.

She told of having a tooth pulled in an effort to get

some attention from her mother, even though there was nothing wrong with the tooth.

In getting her to talk about her sexual background, she described how she had a few experiences with boys her age.

I asked her if she found these early experiences related in any way to her reading problem.

"Oh, yes,"she replied, her face flooding with relief.

"It was something I could do. It was attention-getting."

I asked "Is it possible your reading problem is related to your wanting some attention?"

Linda moaned, wrestling with the question. "It was, as I got older. But if anyone could ever understand this, it wouldn't be worth the price. You don't know what you miss in life by not being able to read.

"I am here because I want to read."

She paused in her story. Her eyes beneath closed lids, then she gripped the arms of the chair determinedly.

"I am a very fine person. I am not stupid. I am going some place with my life. I can feel it. I am going to read some day."

I told Linda—"The crux of your problem is one of self-confidence. You see the root cause of your problems and if you apply yourself you can achieve your goal. But you are going to have to work on your confidence and have faith stronger than your fear. You can achieve what you want to achieve with the technique of self-hypnosis which I will teach you."

Linda relaxed in the reclining chair, smiling slightly.

"Do you feel better?" I asked.

"Yes. I feel better and freer."

In bringing her out of her hypnotic state, I said:

"I want you to forget the negative side of what you have told me. Wipe it out of your mind. It is a new day and time to close the door on your past."

Regression by hypnosis and hypnoanalysis is one of the best ways of remedying a psychological problem of this kind. Through hypnosis and self-hypnosis one can accomplish in a short time, what ordinarily takes months to do with psychotherapy.

In a follow-up of Linda's case I learned she acquired the self-confidence she lacked and was very pleased with the progress she made in overcoming her reading difficulties. She now prides herself in having become an avid reader and having developed a more *positive image* of herself through self-hypnosis.

Frank Capri, a Hollywood-journalist photographer who learned the techniques of self-hypnosis sent me the following:

"The discovery of self-hypnotism and its benefits makes me believe that the next year is going to be a big turning point for me. I'm trying to take it one day at a time here in Hollywood, California. My business of photographing celebrities and professional models is picking up. Self-hypnosis is giving me greater faith, determination, and persistence. Nothing will stop me now. What a joy it is to not only experience more and more success, but to share it along the way. I love the opportunity of helping people in their personal lives and careers. It makes me feel good about myself (positive self-image)."

An actress, Cheryl-Ann Wilson, in Hollywood, California volunteered her personal comments about how she applied *positive thinking* and *self-hypnotic suggestions* to give her the confidence she needed to become successful in her career.

"As an actress in a business which is flooded with competition and rejection, it's important for me to keep my entire outlook *positive*. I suggest to myself that I can succeed regardless of the adversities I encounter. I simply won't *allow* myself to do negative thinking because I know it would make me unhappy and unsuccessful.

"I have an actor friend who has a self-defeating outlook on life. He's allowed people's negative attitudes to seep through into his own attitudes. He feels you have to fight negative with more negative, and of course it's getting him nowhere. It has just made him bitter and difficult to be around."

"He would say to me, 'You'll never make it. You can't have what you want just because you want it.' I said, *'I can have it if I really want it and I'm willing to work for it. Anything I want is within my reach if I can reach far enough.'*

"I believe my success is up to me. And I've seen proof of the power of self-suggestion (self-hypnosis) in my life. As trite as it might sound, when I wake up in the morning I look at it as a brand new day, a day in which fabulous things can happen. I tell myself, *think positive* and *positive results* will follow."

Through self-hypnotism, you can purge yourself of whatever shortcomings and weaknesses you possess.

If you assume a positive attitude about yourself, you will feel at ease around people. If you manifest a positive image of yourself, others will respond favorably to you. People generally relax and feel comfortable listening to a speaker, for instance, who emanates poise and relaxation.

Nevertheless, here are a few liabilities that you can learn to overcome via self-hypnosis.

Chronic Complaining

No one likes to be around someone who is forever complaining about his health.

Self-Centeredness

Egoism is the same as self-centeredness—too much "I." A self-centered individual is constantly thinking about himself. He is egocentric.

Irritability

Avoid being belligerent. Don't go around with a chip on your shoulder. Persons who are easily irritated and oversensitive suffer from an *absence* of a *positive self-image* and project their self-dissatisfaction on to others.

Since hypnosis involves the acceptance of suggestions

based on the premise that we are all "suggestible" you can capitalize on this by influencing people to mutual advantage.

Getting people to like you, to trust you and believe in you comes under the category of *disguised hypnosis.*

You can use unlimited power of hypnotic suggestions to influence others as a force only for good. Your motivation to make people susceptible to suggestions which you implant in their minds must be for their own good.

To project this hypnotic influence onto others there are certain things to keep in mind.

Making a good first impression is important. Before any words are exchanged with a person you meet, you immediately radiate a good or bad impression, depending on how you look. You attract or detract according to your appearance—the way you are dressed. Maximum self-grooming pays dividends. Looking well has a magnetic hypnotic effect on most people.

A smile is another factor. It is an unspoken manifestation of friendliness. The person who smiles is already influencing you hypnotically. Smiling like yawning is *contagious.* You put people in a more *receptive* mood to what you want to tell them. Never underestimate the hypnotic power of a smile.

A calm well-modulated voice also has a magnetic effect on others. The quality of your voice reflects the nature of your personality. For example, a mother singing a soft lullaby to put her baby to sleep comes under the "hypnotic equivalent phenomenon."

Make your voice soothing. Speak slowly. Give your listener a chance to digest what you are saying. Use simple language. Say what you have to say in a pleasing manner. Our ears rebel against a voice that is loud and harsh. When you talk gently you are helping the other person to relax.

Choose your words. Avoid the mistake of offending someone by carelessly speaking without thinking. Be tactful. We are hypnotically attracted to someone who says things we like to hear, who compliments us and who selects a subject of conversation that he knows will interest us. You can keep a person spellbound by what you say and how you say it.

Look people in the eye when you talk to them. Many hypnotists achieve a state of hypnotism in their subjects, staring at them while giving them certain specific suggestions, such as "You are getting drowsy and you will soon be unable to keep your eyes open."

You hold people's attention by looking into their eyes. People can convey their feelings for each other simply by the way they look at one another.

Do everything in a hypnotic, graceful manner. Anything that you do that's done hastily, whether you eat fast, talk fast, walk fast, puts the other person under tension. Slowness in everything you do is more conducive to relaxation.

Manifest a relaxed attitude within yourself. When you are around a person who is very aggressive, loud and wants to dominate the conversation, that's the time you should avoid imitating him. Instead, let him talk himself to a point of embarrassment. Keep yourself on guard prepared for the worst. Keep yourself under control. He will quickly sense your poise before you know it, and will begin to calm down. This is a form of *hypnotism in disguise*. You are influencing him without his knowing it, which is still another form of "hypnotic equivalent."

Radiate confidence. We are all impressed by persons who exude self-confidence. If you suggest to yourself, via self-hypnosis, that you are capable of achieving a certain goal and believe it, you soon learn to project this feeling of self-assurance onto others. You can make a person less afraid if you manifest courage without fear. The inner strength you develop as a result of self-hypnosis can pass on to others.

Be aggressive in a passive way. Many people feel they are making their own decisions about something. Avoid overselling. No one likes to be pressured into buying anything. Make them concentrate on what you would like them to do or consider. Be persuasive, but not over-aggressive.

Select a proper time and place for the use of hypnotic influence. Don't try to influence a person into buying something when he is too busy to talk with you. Take him out to lunch or dinner. Pick out a quiet place. Many business deals have been transacted on a golf course or at a country club over a drink. Dim lights and soft music have helped many men put their women into a romantic mood. The important thing to remember is that true hypnotic influence can be achieved under proper conditions.

Repeat to yourself at varying intervals what you want someone to accept and believe. You can influence people into developing confidence in themselves by letting them know you believe in their capabilities, that they are eventually going to succeed. Inspiring people is equivalent to *hypnotizing* them into a state of confidence.

Make full use of the power of suggestion. Since hypnotism involves the acceptance of suggestion based on the theory that we are all suggestible, we can capitalize on this power of influencing people in this manner. Use the *positive approach.* Tell people that you have confidence in them, that they are more capable than they think—that they are going to succeed, that they can survive whatever setbacks come their way.

Make yourself interesting. You have often heard someone say, "I read such and such a book. It was so interesting I couldn't put it down."

A person will often say, "I could listen to him all night. He's fascinating." This also comes under the category of *Hypnotic Equivalent.*

Display enthusiasm, gesticulate if you have to. Hold the attention of your listener.

Get a person to want to follow your suggestions. It is claimed that hypnosis is often successful because the person who is being hypnotized wants to please the hypnotist. This is partly true.

In getting a person to cooperate, point out the advantages of what you are suggesting that he do. Get him to like you. Make him feel you have his interest at heart, that you are motivated by only one desire—to help him.

Educate—don't scold. No one wants to be constantly criticized or told what's wrong with him.

Teaching someone what he can do to correct a particular fault is wiser than making him feel guilty for having done something wrong. We all like to learn. When you impart knowledge to someone, he likes you. He admires and respects you. Share what you have learned with others.

Make people feel comfortable in your presence. They say big people (celebrities and famous persons) have a way of putting you at ease quickly when you meet them. They magnetize. You can make people feel comfortable in numerous ways, calling them by their first names, getting them to talk about themselves, appearing friendly, shaking hands with them, complimenting them, making them feel you understand their desire to be a friend.

Condition a person's mind to your way of thinking. Example:If you want to encourage your wife to overcome an inferiority complex, tell her at least once a day, that she is manifesting more evidence of self-confidence. Tell her something *positive* about herself each day. Compliment her. Repeat over and over to her the thought that she is capable of improving in every way. She will soon begin to believe this. You are conditioning her mind to positive thinking and a *positive self-image*.

Give the other person something to think about. If you have something you want to tell someone, don't let him get into a debate over it. Suggest that he not comment, but that he digest everything you told him, that he think about it when he is alone, that he sleep on it, as it were.

This gives him an opportunity to absorb more fully the significance of what you are trying to tell him for his own benefit.

Practice the power of hypnotic appeal. Hypnotic appeal is the same as magnetic appeal. It means turning on the charm. Radiating warmth, sincerity, trust and confidence.

Acquaint your friends with the many uses of self-hypnosis. Convince them that *self-hypnotism* is becoming very popular, that people are overcoming undesirable habits with the technique of *self-hypnosis,* that it's also used for such problem conditions as excessive nervousness, shyness, stage fright, fears, insomnia, tension, etc. They will become indebted to you for this helpful knowledge.

Have people visualize what you want them to imagine. It is claimed that hypnotism involves the manipulation of imagination. When you paint a mental picture of something, the person is more likely to be impressed.

Example: "Can you picture yourself driving a beautiful car? Try to imagine what you would look like if you weighed twenty pounds less. Imagine you are a successful salesman. You will soon look like one and act like one."

Use hypnotic influence without making it apparent to others. It consists of getting one's attention fixed on a given idea, and getting the other person to agree with you via an appeal to his emotions, using positive suggestions.

Example: "I'm sure you agree with me that it is better to accept something that you know is good for you—"

You don't have to let the person know you are using *hypnotic techniques*. Getting someone to fall in love with you is another example of disguised hypnosis.

A Summary of a Few Rules to Follow to Influence Others Successfully Through the Power of Suggestion.

- Reflect confidence in what you say.
- Your voice should be soft, firm and appealing.
- Let people conclude quickly that you're poised, and positive in your approach.
- Don't do or say anything that will antagonize your subject.
- Don't give the other person the feeling that you are making up his mind for him.

WHAT CONSTITUTES A "POSITIVE IMAGE"?

The late Dr. Maxwell Maltz, world-famous author of the concept of psycho-cybernetics which has helped millions of people reach a more vital and happier way of life, described a positive self-image as follows:

"It is your conception of your worth, a mental blueprint and internalized self-portrait. When you look at another person, you size up his physical appearance and try to evaluate his characteristics, motives and so on. You appraise yourself in the same fashion and act according to this appraisal; if your evaluation is positive, you will move toward positive goals, while a negative opinion of yourself will steer you toward defeat.

"Tell yourself that you are inferior, unworthy, a failure, and automatically you will trigger off movement toward failure goals.

"See yourself a worthwhile successful deserving person and you are on your way toward constructive goals.

"Thus, you blast off toward richer, fuller living through building a healthy self-image, which is a testimonial to your faith and belief in yourself."

Zelda, an attractive woman in her late forties, became interested in self-hypnotism several years ago. I asked her to describe for me what she considered her "philosophy of life" especially after she informed me how a positive attitude—a belief in herself—helped her cope with various personal problems.

Here is what she wrote:

"A highly intelligent friend, a successful businessman once told me his success was due to his ability to convert every liability into an asset. He was always talking about business, but what he said about the secret of his success impressed me. I began to apply it to my own life. I think about what particular problem I have that is upsetting me, something really worrisome and I try to figure a way to make it a

91

good positive thing rather than a bad and negative thing. Here is a recent example: I bought a new little foreign car last year, and for some reason it didn't hold the road well. The rear end tended to skid out on curves and it "fish-tailed" in wet weather. I'd had it checked, spoke to other owners of that same model—nothing could be found faulty with the car, and no one else seemed to have that problem. I was annoyed and irritated. I just couldn't afford to just go out and buy another car and I didn't feel safe driving the one I had. Finally, a neighbor put four cinder blocks in the trunk which cured the problem by 90 percent. I felt better driving the car but then the cinder blocks annoyed me—they took up so much room.

"Now gardening is my pleasure and my pastime and I consider myself a fair to middling gardener. I have the misfortune to live both in Florida and New York in homes with poor sandy soil. So, when I plant something I dig a hole, discard the sandy soil, fill the hole with topsoil and put the plant in the topsoil and it grows well. The topsoil is not expensive, about $1.50 for forty pounds and it means I have 95 percent success with whatever I plant. Now one day I needed a supply of topsoil, so I took out the four cinder blocks and made room for four bags of topsoil. I didn't get to do the planting for a few days and left the soil in the trunk of the car. I found to my delight, it was just the right weight to make the car handle well. The soil could be pushed in places where the blocks didn't fit due to the flexibility of the plastic bags and it took up much less room. Now I am very happy. I have a car that handles well. I have room in my trunk and I have a constant supply of topsoil. When I use one or two bags, I stop at a hardware store and buy a couple more. If I need every inch of trunk space for baggage to travel north or south I take out the soil and store it under the porch till next season, or sprinkle it over the lawn. I found one little irritation in my life made it into one little pleasure."

Zelda continued with her story:

"On a broader scale, this philosophy has worked for me.

"I was married to a wealthy stockbroker and never really worried about money. We divorced and I found myself with very little income. I am a registered nurse but hadn't worked in that field in twenty years. I was terrified to go back, furious with my ex-husband, my lawyer, his lawyer, etc. for being in this financial position. I was forced to get my courage up, take a refresher at a university and go back to work. It was one of the best things I ever did. I've met wonderful nurses who are friends, and I've had lovely patients. And the world of medicine is so vital—new things all the time. I turned a liability, my lack of friends into an asset, returning to a field of work which has enriched my life—all through self-hypnotic positive thinking.

"I'm working on one small liability right now. The property across from my mobile home is commercial, but it really wasn't used until this year. This year a chain link fence was erected and within the fence are rusting machinery, metal drums, a rusty truck with no rear wheels—piles of shingles— well, a real eyesore. I was very unhappy and annoyed with my new liability. To add to my woes, the prevailing winds carry dust and odor of oil right to my front porch. I gave the situation some thought, found out the owner and went to see him. I explained as tactfully as I could how I felt about my "view" and asked him if he would permit me to plant vines along the fence. I said I would gladly pay for them and I would care for them while I am here. He was a bit vague, but he didn't say "no" so I'll bide my time and go to see him again. I'm hoping to turn the liability of the ugly fence and rusty machinery into an asset of a whole wall of flowering vines. I'm hoping to plant jasmine so that when the breeze blows toward me, there will be a sweet fragrance with it.

"The challenge of my little game is not just to get rid of an annoyance, but to turn it into a pleasure. The idea is to take something negative, but not dwell on the negative aspects. I tell myself in a session of self-hypnotism 'There's got to be something positive here, somewhere, somehow and if I think hard enough I'll figure it out.'

"My philosophy of life of turning a liability into an asset

is really nothing more than positive thinking. I just take one thing at a time, large or small and say 'I just won't let this irritate me, life is too short to be unhappy', and when I really am free of the irritation, a solution to make it an asset seems to come from nowhere. My little game has made my life richer and happier."

CONQUERING YOUR PROBLEMS
THROUGH SELF-HYPNOSIS

Case Illustration

Everyone at one time or another is faced with a problem or problems. Some of them seem insurmountable. At times one wonders how it is possible to survive and continue to go on with life without feeling he or she is being drawn into a pond of quicksand, so to speak.

Your conscious mind tells you: "This is one problem I just can't handle"—or "I can take this only for a short time."

But there is one consoling fact, we have within us the instinct of self-preservation—to survive no matter what. It exists even in animals.

Through self-hypnosis, positive self-given suggestions, we can conquer our problems no matter how serious or long-lasting they seem. We can refuse to sink into the quicksand, and get back on solid ground via self-determination and a positive mental attitude.

Let me cite an example—A patient whom I shall refer to as Rita related the following in her own words:

"My husband's successful business venture of many years duration was wiped out overnight. George (my husband) was told by his doctor that he had cancer and that he also had a serious heart disorder which prohibited him from any kind of activity. His radiation treatments prevented his cancer from spreading. Even though his cancer went into remission, he would repeat over and over again like a broken record:—

94

'My time is up.

'I won't ever get better.

'I will never be able to work again.

'I can't even carry out the simplest chores because of my health problems,' etc. ad infinitum." Rita went on to tell me:

"As a result it was necessary for me to seek employment. Fortunately, I found a job with a book publisher—a job I really enjoyed. It helped me to get away from listening to George's negative thoughts all day long.

"When I came home in the evening, I was so tired that I went to my room to lie down and relax. I not only relaxed physically and mentally, I used self-hypnosis which I had been taught and gave myself positive suggestions—that I would survive and not allow my husband's illness depress me too much.

"Through self-hypnosis I managed to make my problem manageable and endurable without succumbing to a deeper state of mental depression."

I congratulated her and told her to keep surviving as it were.

She knew I was in the process of writing a book "Better Health with Self-Hypnosis" so I asked Rita—"What advice can you give my prospective readers who are experiencing similar problems?"

This is what she wrote:

"Convince yourself that with a positive mental attitude and positive thinking, no problem can destroy you. You have the mind power (combined with a prayer if you so desire) to conquer any problem that you encounter. Don't make the mistake of trying to make your problem less painful and tolerant through alcohol or drugs. They are never the answer to any problem, big or small.

"Practice converting negative thinking into positive thoughts. The words to a song written years ago, "Eliminate the negative and accentuate the positive" still apply today.

"You may not have reason to be happy under certain circumstances, but you can refuse to remain unhappy and depressed.

"Keep in mind that you have the potential of becoming

as strong inside (emotionally) as you want to be and survive despite the circumstances of your particular situational problem."

Summary

1. To acquire a positive self-image, think and act like a winner.
2. A negative self-image is self-destructive.
3. Your mind has unlimited self-healing powers.
4. Self-hypnosis can enable you to surmount obstacles that stand in the way of better health and happiness.
5. A positive mental attitude is indispensable to success.
6. Through self-hypnotism you can eradicate whatever personality weaknesses you possess.
7. Develop hypnotic appeal. Get people to like you.
8. Keep in mind that alcohol and drugs will never be the answer to solving problems.

CHAPTER 6

THE IMPORTANCE OF UNDERSTANDING THE MEANING OF WISDOM, SUCCESS, HAPPINESS, MATURITY AND LOVE

One of the most rewarding assets you can develop is *wisdom*. Your success and happiness in life are dependent on the kind of judgment you exercise choosing your direction in life.

Wisdom is generally attributed to something we acquire in later years—the product of what we have learned from experience.

A person who possesses wisdom is someone who has profited from the past mistakes of his earlier years. But you don't have to wait until you are in the sixth or seventh decade of life to acquire wisdom. Through self-hypnosis you can achieve a better understanding of the real meaning of wisdom—at any age.

If you follow certain specific self-given suggestions, you can enjoy better health and a happier outlook on life.

Give yourself sessions of self-hypnosis as many times as your schedule permits—one, two, or three times a day.

The sessions can vary from a half-hour to an hour. I recommend that you read out loud, if you so desire, the following descriptive sayings re: wisdom. Memorize as many of them as you can, and then proceed to induce your hypnotic state during which repeat to yourself what you recall about what you have learned.

Using this technique over and over again you will condition your mind to what wisdom should mean to you. Specific knowledge of this kind can definitely change your lifestyle for the better. It will prevent you from becoming self-destructive. Keep in mind that health-dissipations and wisdom are incompatible.

During your sessions of self-hypnosis, repeat the following:

* Wisdom means never allowing myself to lose my zest for living.
* It means a determination to survive personal sorrows and disappointments.

* Wisdom means reminding myself that tactfulness, kindness and usefulness are self-rewarding—that it is better to love than to hate.
* Wisdom also means experiencing pride and happiness in the joy of accomplishments.
* Wisdom means believing in myself convincing myself that I *can* instead of I *can't*. As Dryden said: "They can conquer who believe they can."
* Wisdom means self-discipline, the refusal to be overcome by needless worries and fears.
* Wisdom refers to tolerance and compassion for my fellow man. It includes self-acceptance with the conviction that happiness is a state of mind.
* It means a willingness to make necessary sacrifices and assume responsibilities knowing that I can never solve my problems by running away from them.
* Wisdom is a reminder that the things that are the most worthwhile are often the hardest to achieve.
* Wisdom means making time to enjoy life.
* Wisdom means doing unto others as I would expect them to do unto me.
* Wisdom means being able to accept constructive criticism wisely.
* Wisdom means learning by listening.
* Wisdom means having people accept me for what I am rather than what I pretend to be.
* Finally, wisdom means the courage to defend my ideals.

By applying the above to day-to-day living via self-hypnotism, your mode of living and thinking is bound to improve in every way.

SUCCESS

As you might suspect success means different things to different individuals. However, there are things you can suggest to yourself regarding the meaning of success that can influence you in your sense of values and contribute to better health, fulfillment of your goals, and enjoyment of life.

Follow the same instructions as you just did for the acquisition of wisdom. You can similarly condition your mind with the following self-given suggestions.

* Success entails organized thinking, successful self-management, wise planning—making the most of your potentials.
* Success is something that begins with my inner self—a feeling of self-confidence, a willingness to do my best in anything I undertake.
* Success means the development of self-discipline, making self-improvement a way of life.
* Success means perseverance, being a "doer" instead of a "dreamer."
* Success implies developing a mature sense of values, health-intelligence, doing everything in moderation, living in balance.
* Success means prosperity, economic security combined with integrity.
* Success includes self-respect.
* Success means being optimistic, with faith in myself, and in a Higher Power.
* Success is peace of mind, serenity, inner happiness and self-satisfaction.
* Success is reverence for life, a love of mankind.
* Success means using time wisely.
* Success means adherence to a code of ethics. Success means self-discovery, getting along with others, becoming the kind of person I want to be.
* It is also the ability to love, accept love, and share love.
* Success is the refusal to be unhappy—I am the master of my fate and life with all its imperfections and complications is worth the price of surviving.

Now that you have a deeper appreciation of the meaning of wisdom and success, you can further benefit by devel-

100

oping a better understanding of the meaning of happiness, maturity, and love.

There are millions of men and women today who have little conception or a distorted notion of what constitutes maturity, how one finds happiness and what love in or out of wedlock entails. As a consequence, our divorce rate is on the increase and so many of us, because of our immaturity, choose lifestyles that are detrimental to our physical and mental well-being.

Ignorance is no excuse for failure and unhappiness. Decide that you are going to teach yourself what you need to learn about happiness, maturity, and love and apply that knowledge, utilizing the technique of self-hypnotism as you did with wisdom and success. Make this particular chapter especially important. Make it the *key to self-improvement.*

HAPPINESS

Happiness is a *positive self-hypnotic* attitude of mind. Happiness is the ability to survive misfortunes. Happiness is growing wiser instead of older. Happiness is freedom from fear. Happiness is the absence of hatred and prejudice. Happiness is fortitude. Happiness is self-improvement. Happiness is the joy of accomplishments. Happiness is unselfishness, respect, and consideration for others. Happiness is forgiveness, kindness, and tolerance. Happiness is self-understanding. Happiness is giving and helping others. Happiness is the science and art of enjoying life. Happiness is humility. Happiness is believing in oneself. Happiness is maturity. Happiness is successful living. Happiness is love of oneself and love of life. Happiness is faith in a higher power within ourselves, in mankind and in the goodness and purpose of life. Happiness is an appreciation of all that is beautiful and meaningful. Happiness is a willingness to make it a better world for all of us. Happiness is *self-hypnotic positive thinking.*

Dr. Frank G. Slaughter in his book "Your Body And

Your Mind" stated, "We strive to be healthy in order to be happy but how many of us strive to be happy in order to be healthy?"

It is negative thinking that causes people to be unhappy. You can create your own peace of mind and happiness utilizing what you have learned about techniques of self-hypnotism.

Apropos of the concept of happiness—I was surprised to discover that a friend of mine, Richard Eton, had written a self-help book entitled "Work Wonders From Within Yourself."

He also operated a radio station for a good many years. His talks on the air were considered gems of wisdom that served as self-education therapy for his listeners.

It is gratifying to learn that he concurs with me regarding the value of *mind power* and the need for our own enjoyment of life.

Here are some of his inspirational excerpts to keep in mind during your sessions of hypnotic self-therapy:

* When we choose to be, we are the masters of our minds and of our lives.
* We can control our reactions—and when our reactions are based on love and compassion, we cannot fail to lead a better and happier life.
* It is you who decides whether some unfortunate event fills you with worry, despair and defeat—or whether you carry on with faith, courage, appreciation, love, and all else that turns seeming defeat into real and wonderful victory.
* As you practice to lead a happy successful life, you help to bring happiness and success to many others.
* There is nothing in your life that cannot be changed, corrected, or alleviated by changing your attitude.
* No problem is bigger than you, and you carry the solution to all your problems within yourself.
* Make a habit out of optimistic thinking, and gradually and wonderfully an automatically optimistic view takes over.
* Our world is our thinking.

MATURITY

In my 37 years of practice as a psychiatrist, I have witnessed a tragic amount of unhappiness caused by *immaturity*. There is no doubt that many divorces, for example, that resulted from marital misery might have been prevented had the husband and wife entered marriage with an adequate understanding of the meaning of maturity.

Maturity is not something you are born with. It is something that can be acquired and developed through *self-hypnosis*.

A mature person has a *positive image* of himself as described in a previous chapter. He is tolerant and free of prejudices, has an open mind and is able to forgive when necessary. He makes himself companionable and cooperative and avoids complications that are detrimental to his physical and emotional well-being. He has a sense of humor and gets his problems in focus, is generous and willing to help others, lives in moderation, practices self-discipline, and creates his own happiness. He is capable of accepting and sharing love. He survives setbacks and has faith in himself and mankind.

Maturity is the capacity to think and act as a well-integrated adult. It is being able to have developed a detached relationship to parents—to accept reality—to assume responsibilities and manifest evidence of being self-sustaining. Maturity comes from personality growth and development. It implies emotional stability.

A mature man or woman possesses wisdom and tactfulness and has a healthy sense of values. He or she is able to adapt successfully to changing situations, to be flexible and not rigid in thinking, has a congenial disposition and is easy to get along with; and to be an optimist and not a pessimist.

Maturity means profiting from past mistakes, achieving a balanced way of life which makes living enjoyable instead of painful. A mature individual is glad to be alive—has

103

learned to relax and is inspired by a personal philosophy of life—that life is what one makes it.

Maturity means adapting to a system of thinking based on an appreciation of all that is beautiful for peace of mind and the joy of living.

THE MEANING OF LOVE

What is Love?

Love is living. Love is giving. Love is warmth. Love is being alive, a *joie de vivre*. Love is courage. Love is wisdom. Love is understanding. Love is forgiveness. Love is kindness. Love is protection, security, belonging. Love is acceptance. Love is togetherness. Love is an appreciation of beauty. Love is creative self-expression. Love is a sharing of laughter. Love is happiness. Love is emotional and sexual maturity. Love is building, growing, believing. Love is loving. Love is a reason for living. Love is life's fulfillment.

Gerald G. Jampolsky, in his recently published book *Teach Only Love* (Bantam Books 1983) describes the meaning of love as follows:

"Love is total acceptance and total giving—with no boundaries and no exceptions. Love, being the only reality, cannot be transformed. It can only extend and expand. It unfolds endlessly and beautifully upon itself. Love sees everyone as blameless, it recognizes the light within each of us. Love is the total absence of fear and the basis for all *attitudinal healing*."

Incidentally, his book points out the interrelationship between love and attitudinal healing. He claims that "Our attitudes determine whether we experience peace or fear, whether we are well or sick."

This premise substantiates how a *positive mental attitude* using techniques of *self-hypnosis* influences one's convalescence from illness and physical symptoms (see Chapter 4).

PARENTING AND SELF-HYPNOSIS

Parents today are traditionally threatened by their children as they emerge into the teen years. It is in those years that young people suddenly view the older generation as narrow, dogmatic, and not a little absurd. No longer are parents respected as founts of wisdom. They are accused of being "squares" who fail to understand the problems of younger people.

Young adults merit all the time and energy that parents and society can spare them. Though they covet independence they are still dependent on their parents—emotionally as well as financially. Parents need to keep this in mind. How teenagers think and what they do have a tremendous impact on society as a whole and affect their parents for good or ill. They can disturb the peace of a home and divide parents against each other.

At a White House Conference on Children, it was concluded that healthy personality development in children depends in large measure on the character of parents' attitudes and the nature of the parent-child relationship.

Becoming a mature, healthy parent is not simple. It requires effort. Through self-hypnosis you can definitely develop greater love and understanding between yourself and your children.

The following are some self-given suggestions you can give yourself during sessions of self-hypnotism.

Session No. I

* Self-understanding is the first step to a better relationship with my children.
* I am going to ask myself while in a self-hypnotic state . . . .
* What personality traits do I have which interfere with my being a good parent?
* How did I acquire these negative elements in my personality?

* Are my children a problem only because I have never been able to understand my own emotions?
* Why do I react the way I do toward my children?
* Am I unhappily married and taking it out on my children?
* Am I disappointed in myself and making my children the scapegoat victims of my frustrations?
* Do I give them too much freedom to do as they wish?
* Am I too strict?
* Do I give them the required amount of love, affection, and encouragement?
* Do I have the tendency to blame them when I really should be blaming myself?

Self-analysis of this kind will enable you to develop insight to yourself. You'll know what shortcomings as a parent you need to correct. Proceed to follow the specific self-given suggestions during subsequent sessions of self-hypnosis.

Incidentally, many parents prefer not to learn about themselves. The process can turn out to be painful and everyone wants to avoid discomfort. You are to be commended if you are willing to examine yourself in relation to your children.

Session No. 2

* I am going to avoid extremes. If I vacillate from being an overly strict disciplinarian to being overly permissive, I may cause my children to become confused.
* I am going to become firm, but kind. Educating them to want to improve themselves is better than scolding.

Session No. 3

* I am not going to express unhappiness in relation to my husband or wife in the presence of my children. It will only make them feel insecure and cause them to become disillusioned.

* I am going to keep my emotions under control when communicating with my children. Outbursts of anger and shouting make everything worse.

Session No. 4

* I am going to take time to know my children—to share their problems—and to share their joys as well.
* I am never going to be too busy to listen to them. They crave affection and companionship.
* I am going to give them the feeling they are loved—that I will try to be forgiving and understanding.

Session No. 5

* I am going to help my children grow and achieve emotional maturity. I will set a good example for them.
* I will give them an opportunity to make independent decisions.
* I am going to avoid giving them the impression that I "own them." At the same time I am going to guard against children becoming too dependent on me for everything. I am going to compliment them when they do something well.

Session No. 6

* I will never "write off," as it were, my children. It may drive them to drugs, alcohol, or suicide. Self-hypnosis entails forgiveness.
* I am going to convince myself that becoming a good parent is as important as anything else in life.

Session No. 7

* I am willing to admit that I may need counseling and will seek it. I am not going to let false pride keep me from getting professional help. Money spent on getting help for my children is money spent wisely.

Concluding Reminder

Keep in mind that the successful management of your children means balancing love and discipline—firmness with kindness—understanding and forgiveness.

CHAPTER 7

DEVELOPING MORE ENERGY— OVERCOMING NERVOUS TENSION, FATIGUE AND DEPRESSION

Nervous tension affects not only physical health, but mental health. It deprives you of much-needed energy and vitality.

Many people claim they have been nervous all of their lives. We are all capable of being tense and fearful under special circumstances, of lacking self-confidence at times and worrying needlessly about what may happen to us.

The solution to *nervous tension* is to learn to *relax*. You must convince yourself that you *can* relax. Relaxation is something you *learn,* just as you learn to spell and read. It is a misconception that if you are uptight and nervous and tense you are always going to be that way.

In his book, Dr. Walter C. Alvarez (Live At Peace With Your Nerves) advocates naps for people who wish to relax and relieve themselves of tension. Even ten minutes will suffice, he says, recommending a nap after lunch. I for one, have taken a midday nap and was more relaxed getting more done than if I allowed myself to keep going without respite.

In an issue of *National Enquirer,* reporter Chuck Michelini described how Abby Dalton, a star of "Falcon Crest," uses self-hypnosis to cope with stress and tension.

"I've been using self-hypnosis since a friend of mine taught me how, Abby confided in an exclusive interview. "It's helped tremendously in my private life." For example she overcame her insomnia and learned to achieve a state of total relaxation.

When Abby feels "uptight" and tense, she heads for her dressing room during her lunch break and "hypnotizes" herself to go to sleep for about an hour—then wakes up "totally refreshed."

Here is how she relieves herself of tension.

"I lie down on the floor, place my legs on a chair and my head on a pillow. Then I start relaxing my body from the toes to my head. The tension just seems to flow from my body. And if I want to sleep, I can be out in 18 seconds flat using this technique.

"When I want to rid myself of a painful headache, I start off with the same relaxation exercise, then I go one step further.

"Once my body is totally relaxed, I conjure up an image of the most beautiful place I know—a small spot up in the High Sierra, which to me is the most beautiful place on earth.

"In my mind's eye, I project myself to this spot. And after 5 to 10 minutes of this, the pain begins to subside significantly. That simple exercise helps me control the pain until the headache goes away.

"Whenever the pressures start to creep in at home, I just practice self-hypnosis until the stress and tension are relaxed."

She adds: "I'm a firm believer in everyone trying it. It's simple, quick and doesn't cost a dime. For me, it's been a life-saver at times."

If you keep telling yourself you are relaxed, eventually you will be. It is simply a *conditioned habit.* Tell yourself "My how relaxed I feel," until you really are.

Forgiving relieves tension. Learn to forgive and forget.

Act happy and you will grow into the role. It will cause you to think of reasons to be happy—to justify your going around acting happy. You will discover inadvertently that you have much to be happy about.

Laughter is a tension-reliever. It's an emotional tranquilizer.

NERVOUS FATIGUE

Many patients who consult doctors today complain of chronic tiredness which is a body-mind reaction far more prevalent than the common cold. Our modern tempo of living, and the chaotic conditions throughout the world are contributing factors.

There are many of us who strive to keep going without giving our bodies the necessary chance to recuperate. Some

111

of us complain of constantly feeling exhausted and cannot account for the source of our fatigue. We experience exaggerated tiredness, insomnia, irritability, and a host of physical ailments–headaches, digestive disorders, vague aches and pains, difficulty in concentrating, and disinclination to work.

If you were driving at night and you began to swerve off the road because you were tired and sleepy, you would realize that it would be only sensible to stop and rest.

The person who risks a nervous breakdown is usually an individual who refuses to pause physically and mentally. He can be compared to someone who drives himself to the point of falling asleep at the wheel. The crash that follows is the result of his accumulated fatigue. Often, the crash comes before he realizes its approach.

Excessive fatigue is a form of chemical intoxication that affects the entire nervous system and in turn alters the mental disposition of the individual. You become fatigue-drunk. With adequate rest the fatigue poisons are eliminated and you become "sober."

There are millions of people in this predicament, helpless because they have never been taught how to slow down and relax.

Paul boasts of how busy he keeps himself at his place of business. When he comes home he is peevish, complains to his wife that he is "worn out." He wonders why he doesn't get a raise in salary. His error is in thinking that keeping frantically busy means working efficiently. Unfortunately, Paul hasn't learned the secret of economizing his energy and doing things in a relaxed way.

DEPRESSION

How much do you really know about this particularly severe emotional problem?

35 million Americans suffer from depression. Depres-

sion is a term that covers conditions ranging from simple sadness, through grief, to utter despair.

But depression becomes serious when it lingers for a long time. For instance, if your depression due to a loss of a loved one doesn't lift after three months, you may have a problem that needs attention. Or if there is no apparent reason for your depression, you should seek professional help.

What are the *symptoms* of serious depression? Irritability, a sense of hopelessness, lack of interest in everything, sleep disorders, profound feelings of worthlessness, and thoughts of suicide,

Some deeply depressed individuals refuse to leave the house. Others sleep all day. Still others stop caring about cleanliness or lose desire for food.

What Causes Depression?

It can be caused by a chemical imbalance in the brain. This type can be treated by antidepressant drugs. They take several weeks or more to elevate a depressed person's moods. Others drugs are prescribed for chronically depressed individuals who oversleep and overeat.

Hereditary predisposition can also cause depression in some cases—people who grew up in a family that was predisposed to be gloomy or where the parents were depressed, are more likely to suffer from depression themselves.

What Can You Do About Depression?

Self-hypnosis can help you develop positive thinking. Read self-help literature and apply what you have learned. Get your mind off yourself. Become involved in anything that interests you.

Exercise is another way to lift your spirits. It tones up muscles, improves circulation, invigorates and enlivens you. You need to change your routine to get out of the depression habit.

Can Depression Be Cured?

Definitely. According to Dr. Bruce J. Roansville, Assistant Professor of Psychiatry at Yale University School of Medicine–"Because of advances in treatment, self-help, psychotherapy and drugs, 80 percent of people suffering from depression do get better."

HOW TO PREVENT A NERVOUS BREAKDOWN
WITH SELF-HYPNOSIS

A nervous breakdown is a state in which certain emotional conflicts interfere with one's ability to continue the normal routine of living.

Persons who had a bad start in life are more apt to get hurt when they encounter a serious frustration in later life. They generally suffer from two conflicts—the root conflict that deals with a childhood frustration, arising out of a bad relationship with their parents and an actual conflict which consists of some precipitating factor such as a major disappointment, loss of money, the death of a dear one, job worries, failure at school or college, and illness. They are not the true causes of breakdowns, but they help to precipitate them.

We all know of individuals who have been exposed to all sorts of adversities, yet have stood up to them well. Others are emotionally incapacitated by them. It is the combination of inner weakness or predisposition plus the precipitating factors that causes the ultimate breakdown.

At any rate, nervous breakdowns can be prevented. It requires an ability to live in balance. Most important for nervous and mental stability is the ability to channel our thinking along normal, healthy lines. Our lives can be no better than our thoughts. Because we are living in a civilized world, we have learned that for happy living together we must repress certain desires that are natural to human beings. When we continue to secretly harbor these desires, they often find expression in psychosomatic health complaints.

Ted had been a serious-minded business man most of his life. He confessed that he had no interest in pleasures and pastimes. He claimed he couldn't take vacations because of his commitment to his business. His wife Joan informed me that she feared he was on the verge of a breakdown. He lost his sense of humor, worried about paying off the mortgage on his home and suffered from depression and chronic fatigue.

Joan requested that I consider the possibility of hypnotizing him, hoping, of course, that he would take a healthier attitude about himself.

Ted became a willing subject for hypnosis. He realized his health was failing him. His doctor concluded that physically there was no reason for him to feel tired and depressed. Ted admitted that he was bored—that he had always been a chronic worrier even prior to marrying.

Hypnosis enabled Ted to learn the technique of self-relaxation which he practiced twice a day—once in the morning and again at bedtime. During his sessions of hypnosis he agreed his symptoms of unhappiness and depression corroborated the diagnosis that he was a casualty of what is known as the "Burnout Syndrome."

Here is what he reported following hypnotherapy.

* I am using self-given suggestions and telling myself that I am experiencing a complete transformation of my personality.
* Self-hypnosis has inspired in me a zest for life which I never had before.
* I feel I have discovered a new image of myself.
* After work hours I enjoy and share a happy-hour Martini with my wife.
* I have planned to take a Caribbean cruise which is long overdue.
* I am teaching myself that chronic worrying is a self-curable habit as you pointed out.

115

* When I hypnotize myself I remind myself that life is to be enjoyed.
* I feel like an entirely new person—that I have found myself, so to speak, and that I am just beginning to live.

In another instance, Lorna, a wealthy widow, had been referred to me because of fear that she was on the verge of a mental collapse. Her complaint symptoms were feelings of self-discontent, weariness, loneliness, living in the past, and a loss of interest in everything.

Her doctor called me and informed me over the phone that she was in good physical health. He attributed her state of depression to the fact that she was never able to adjust emotionally to the death of her husband.

Lorna, during one of her sessions of hypnosis, claimed she was only half-alive and was convinced she would never be happy again. I explained to Lorna that to be unhappy temporarily considering the circumstances was normal, but to remain unhappy indefinitely was abnormal—that chronic unhappiness is an illness and as such is curable.

I recommended that she put into practice the technique of self-hypnosis—that she give herself the following suggestions:

* I am going to assume a healthier attitude toward myself.
* I don't have to be lonely—loneliness is self-created.
* I have the advantage of being financially independent for which I am grateful.
* I am going to assume a new lease on life, make new friends, and convince myself that happiness is a state of mind.
* Each morning when I give myself a session of self-hypnosis I am going to tell myself that today is a new beginning, a new chance to make each day an interesting one.
* I am going to conquer negative thoughts and acquire a positive image of myself.
* As Dr. Caprio taught me, the management of life begins with inner contentment—self-happiness.

* I am going to recapture what I once had, a will to survive and enjoy life.

* I am going to remind myself during each session of self-hypnotism that dwelling on the past is equivalent to chasing butterflies in a cemetery—that I'm determined to practice positive thinking regarding whatever the future holds for me.

At her last session of hypnosis I typed out for her on a 3 × 5 card—to carry in her purse at all times—the following:

> If we are ever to enjoy life, now is the time, not tomorrow or next year, or in some future life after we have died. The best preparation for a better life next year is a full, completely harmonious, joyous life this year. Our beliefs in a rich future life are of little importance unless we coin them into a rich present life. Today should always be our most wonderful day.

Convince yourself that you can survive all of life's problems and frustrations that come your way whether you have caused them or others have caused them.

Life with all its complications is still worth living and surviving.

Tell yourself that you do not need to have a breakdown. Use self-hypnosis as often as you need to. It makes it possible to go through life letting your intellect's positive thinking triumph over your emotions and negative thinking—finding happiness within yourself.

Tell yourself also that each time you get a negative thought you are going to substitute a positive thought for it. Refuse to let your mind rule you. Learn to rule your mind instead.

RECOMMENDATIONS

Don't waste your life regretting past mistakes. Keep looking ahead. Avoid arguments. Intelligent individuals reason things out.

Don't become high-geared, sensitive, irritable, subject to outbursts of temper. Learn to be tolerant, cooperative, and above all, cheerful. Remember controlling your emotions means conserving your energy.

Develop the art of relaxation. Work in rhythm by learning to do things well in the easiest way. You relax while dancing or else you are an awkward dancer. Why not learn to relax while working? Remember, too, that haste makes waste. Take things in their natural stride. An interval rest period when possible is helpful. It gives your mind a breathing spell. Don't talk shop during lunch hour. When you come home, forget what happened at the office. Learn to lock your troubles in your desk drawer with your unfinished work. Feed your mind with pleasant thoughts. It relaxes tired nerves.

Counteract occupational boredom. Working at something you don't particularly like, or are not fitted for, gives rise to mental stagnation. If you must continue at your job because of its compensations or because no other job is available, then plan your recreation to recover from the monotony of the work. If yours is a sitting job, seek your recreation in tennis, golf, swimming, dancing, or biking. If your job requires constant use of your arms and legs, then seek recreation through Bridge, the theatre, automobile riding, or reading a book. It isn't because you spend eight hours a day working that you are exhausted. It is because you exercise the same few muscles all day with neglect to the other muscles of your body. The monotony of routine living—doing the same thing day in and day out—coming home, eating, feeling sluggish, and going to bed early is apt to make you a casualty of mental exhaustion.

Use recreation as psychological medicine. This does not mean that you must play every day and every weekend. Some hours must be spent in personal chores. But some diversion every week is desirable. Often, planning for that trip, that party or that sport brings as much pleasure and relaxation as the event itself.

Check with your doctor. If after a checkup with your doctor, no evidence can be found of any illness and overwork is not a factor, then you may safely conclude your tension and fatigue are due to psychological causes.

Keep mentally healthy. Keep your mind relaxed and free of any unpleasantness that tended to keep you upset. Emotional disturbances can tire one more quickly than physical labor.

Learn to budget your energy. Conserve your energy if you wish to enjoy better health. Screen star Stefanie Powers informs us that—"Energy is the most valuable thing you have. If your energy is up, you can accomplish anything. Energy is your life force. If you realize how much energy you dissipate in frustration, anguish, and psychological problems you won't waste it on meaningless things or on people who will deplete you of energy."

CHAPTER 8

SEX HEALTH: HOW TO REMEDY SEXUAL INADEQUACY

There is *good health* and *poor health*. Likewise, there is *sex health* and sex sickness. Sex has a direct influence on your physical and mental well-being. Sex is intimately related to your glandular system, which in turn affects all the organs of your body. It influences your personality and overall outlook on life.

It is a fallacy to believe that your physical health has little to do with your sex life. As a matter of fact chronic tiredness and a general run-down condition may act as predisposing factors in the development of sex dissatisfaction. What you do to improve your sex life also contributes to the improvement of your physical health.

John, age 53, sought counseling because of his wife's indifference to sex. Here is what he described in writing:

"Mary has complained about her health ever since the day we were married. She must be what doctors call a 'hypochondriac.' During our married years I have wanted sex so many times but was unable to discuss the matter without her becoming resentful. She rebuffed me most of the time. It was either, 'I'm tired' or 'I have a terrible headache' or 'My stomach is acting up again.' She has used health excuses more times than I can remember. Many husbands would have looked outside for satisfaction. I haven't. She never met me halfway in sex. She tells me she has to be in the mood and that she has always been inhibited since she was a teenager. All she thinks about are her ailments. Even her doctor told me that most of her complaints have no physical basis. He has given her tranquilizers but she says 'They don't help too much.'"

Fortunately, Mary was convinced to accept help. She responded to hypnosis and learned to apply *self-hypnosis*. It made all the difference in the world. Her enjoyment of sex for the first time enabled her to feel a hundred percent better, physically and mentally.

Everyone is involved in one way or another with sexuality. Some participate and gratify their desires. Others prefer to repress them or try to sublimate their pent-up sexual energy. To be realistic, you can't be "bottled up" sexually and not pay a price. To deny sex is to *dehumanize* yourself. People should remind themselves that sexual fulfillment is an all-embracing *body-mind* experience. It adds to the joy of existence.

Many sexually frustrated couples need nothing more than re-education in the art of sexual lovemaking.

Sex sickness and poor physical health often go together. Sex health on the other hand, represents two bodies and two minds sharing a joyous, delightful harmony. It is a sweeping away of tensions, conflicts, and despairs. It is a gathering in of the most ecstatic kind of living and loving.

Sexuality entails a person's need to feel love. To give love, to share love. It involves one's total self—one's total ego. It is synonymous with body-soul communication. In lovemaking you are making love with your *mind* as well as with your sex organs.

All human beings have a built-in sex love drive. It satisfies a biological and emotional need. Without it, there would be no human race.

Edward O'Relly who holds an MA degree in psychology and philosophy from McGill University, Montreal, Canada informs us:

> Your sex drive affects your nervous system, your circulatory system, your respiratory system, your digestive system, your excretory system, your muscular system, and your endocrine system as well as your reproductive system. It could not be otherwise, because your sex glands empty their products of internal secretion directly into your blood stream, which serves every cell, tissue, organ, and systems that make up your entire body. It is impossible to divorce your sex drive from your body as a whole because it is an inherent part of it from birth to death, and influences everything you think or feel or do.

In my experience as a psychotherapist and marriage counselor I often suspected that when a couple decided to dissolve a marriage because of money quarrels, in-law inter-ference, or some personality clash, the love relationship was probably a poor one to begin with. In many cases there ex-isted a problem of sexual disharmony. What can you expect from a marriage that was lacking in both love and sexual gratification?

It is my opinion that a person who has a sexual problem can with *self-hypnosis* achieve sexual fulfillment. I realize that there are those who suffer from sexual disorders that are deep-seated and require the services of a competent psychotherapist. If you have come to the conclusion that you need the help of a psychiatrist, marriage counselor, or psy-chologist, then by all means avail yourself of this special help.

If you undertake therapy from someone, you can still profit from the knowledge contained in this book. Learning the technique of self-hypnosis will make you a more recep-tive and cooperative student.

There is no excuse today for not doing something about a sexual problem. We know more about the psychology of love and sex than ever before. This information is accessible to everyone. All you need is a willingness to apply what you can learn. To suffer from a sexual problem isn't too difficult to understand. But to remain sexually unhappy only because you refuse to educate yourself or to seek professional help is uncondonable.

The trend now is a do-it-yourself sex-health program. Self-hypnosis enables you to achieve self-discipline, which is necessary to effect a cure.

As you have learned by now, self-hypnosis utilizes the power of your subconscious mind. You will acquire the mind power and self-confidence to solve any problem you have.

Start with the attitude that you *can,* you *must* and you *will* solve your sex problem with self-hypnosis. Assume the attitude that you are not going to become discouraged, that you can apply the technique of self-hypnosis (positive self-communication) that will ultimately achieve your goal so long as you are determined and persistent.

Before you start self-hypnosis teach yourself to relax.

Make relaxation a *habit*. Remind yourself that you are going to think and do everything in a relaxed way. Your mind must become accustomed to relaxing before it can become receptive to self-hypnotic suggestion.

Self-induced relaxation is the *secret* of self-induced hypnosis. It prepares the way to communicate with your subconscious mind. When you are in a hypnotically induced state of relaxation, you are ready to tackle and resolve your particular sexual problem.

Years ago, I decided to use hypnosis in the treatment of sexual disorders. The results were encouraging. In the hypnotic state patients were able to recall experiences in their childhood and adolescence that contributed to the development of their particular sexual problems. Hypnosis enabled them to feel comfortable talking about their intimate experiences and thus able to get to the roots of their problems. In many cases, they acquired sufficient insight to bring about their own improvement.

Incidentally, it might be interesting to know that the use of hypnosis for the treatment of sexual problems goes back 80 years. Both Dr. von Schrenck Noting and Havelock Ellis wrote about *hypnosis* and *sexual problems*.

I might add that insight-therapy does not guarantee a cure. It must be supplemented with sex-education via reading authoritative books on the subject.

Most sexual problems are *psychological* in origin. Consequently, they must be treated with *psychological methods*.

Frances, the mother of three children became hysterical and suffered a nervous breakdown when she learned that her husband had been unfaithful. She decided to sue for a divorce. Her doctor referred her to me for treatment. I gave her several sessions of hypnosis and taught her the technique of self-hypnosis. I also interviewed the husband who assured his wife that his infidelity was circumstantial and not planned. He promised to break off his relationship with the other woman. The ultimate result was a favorable one.

Frances forgave her husband, recovered from her breakdown, and by her own admission became a more responsive marital partner. Don, her husband, had complained that she had previously rejected him on numerous occasions. Sex had become infrequent and minus the enthusiasm she once displayed during the early years of their marriage.

The adequate solution to your problem consists of 1) acquainting yourself with the latest scientific facts about your specific problem, 2) analyzing yourself and acquiring insight into the factors in your past life that led to the development of your problem, 3) tell yourself over and over again during self-hypnosis what you need to believe and accept via self-given suggestions, 4) keeping a record of your progress and reinforcing your self-confidence with as many additional sessions of self-hypnosis as you require. Strong motivation together with acquired self-understanding effects a cure and enables you to achieve sexual maturity.

WHAT TO TELL YOURSELF

- That sexual fulfillment is essential to good health and a happy marriage.
- That sexual unhappiness can have a serious detrimental influence on my personality.
- That sexual information gained from reading authoritative books dealing with every aspect of sexual expression is a step in the right direction.
- That the sex act should be a body-soul expression of love.
- That sexual problems of impotence, frigidity, incompatibility in marriage, and other problems are curable.
- That it is unwise for me to remain sexually unhappy without doing something about it.
- That it is wiser to avoid anything that will lead to such complications as infidelity, promiscuity, etc.

- That I cannot hope to attain sexual maturity as long as I harbor prejudices, misconceptions, or guilt feelings based on past unpleasant experiences.
- That anything I do within reason to enhance my sexual happiness in marriage is normal.
- That it is possible to cure my particular sexual problem via self-education, self-analysis, self-discipline, and self-hypnosis.

SEXUAL INCOMPATIBILITY

It is estimated that problems of sexual incompatibility exist in at least half of all marriages. Some investigators claim that not one marriage in ten has a satisfactory sexual relationship and that the majority of divorces are without a doubt caused by sexual incompatibility.

FRIGIDITY

How do we define frigidity? It is an overall term for *sexual inadequacy* in the female. It does not necessarily imply sexual coldness or sexual indifference. Frigidity is an unfortunate term because many women harbor various misconceptions regarding the real meaning of the term. It is a complex problem insofar as a woman may desire sex, be passionate, find the sex act pleasant, and still suffer from frigidity. It is actually a symptom disorder in the psychosexual development of women, causing them to find it difficult to achieve an orgasm during intercourse.

Frigidity may occur among women who are unable to experience an orgasm because their husbands are clumsy and awkward or are unable to sustain an erection or suffer from premature or hasty ejaculation. Very often when the husband's potency is restored, the wife is able to experience sexual satisfaction.

In some cases sexual unresponsiveness is caused by inhibitions, false modesty, or sexual ignorance. With *self-hypnosis* and proper re-education of attitudes the capacity to achieve orgasm can be developed.

Irene who had been taught the technique of self-hypnosis, cured herself of her frigidity through *hypno-suggestive self-therapy,* and began experiencing orgasms for the first time, much to the delight of her husband.

> When I had my first orgasm, I had a feeling of well-being, self-assurance and intense pleasure of being with my husband. I had a vivid awareness of the world, its beauty and exhilarated feeling of wanting to enjoy life. I felt alive. I even felt I had become prettier and more attractive after having an orgasm. I've looked in a mirror and noticed a change of expression on my face—one of happiness and satisfaction.

If you have any doubts as to whether self-education will help you cure yourself of frigidity, here is what Dr. Marie Robinson wrote in her preface to her book *The Power of Sexual Surrender*: "Women who suffer from frigidity generally know very little about their problem. They do not know its nature or its causes or know how or where to find it."

Blanche, an attractive woman in her late thirties, was referred to me by her doctor because she complained of constant headaches and pains that could not be attributed to any physical cause. The doctor had tried various medications, hoping to relieve her of her symptoms. He concluded she was suffering from some emotional problem and recommended that she subject herself to a psychiatric evaluation.

Under hypnosis, Blanche disclosed that she had engaged in several extra-marital affairs. She considered herself "oversexed" and could not help herself. She pretended all during marriage that she experienced an orgasm every time she had relations with her husband, Carl. When she became intimate with other men, she realized that she was unable to achieve sex satisfaction. She was informed during hypnosis that her symptoms were the result of her subconscious feeling of guilt and that her frigidity or difficulty in experiencing an orgasm accounted for her infidelity.

Many sexually frustrated women who are unable to achieve an orgasm during intercourse become promiscuous in order to learn whether the next partner would give them satisfaction. Despite the fact that they met with repeated disappointments, they found sex relations with other men pleasurable.

After learning the technique of hypnotizing herself, she explored the possible cause of her frigidity problem and was able to achieve sufficient insight to improve her responsiveness to her husband's lovemaking.

The success of hypnosis and self-hypnosis lies in the fact that you can get at the *root* of the sexual problem within a short time. Most husbands and wives respond successfully to self-hypnosis. One can only base the success of self-hypnosis on what the patients report. They are not going to claim beneficial results unless they experience them. It is inconceivable for a man who avails himself of hypnosis combined with self-hypnosis to report that he has been able to achieve a satisfactory result if he hasn't.

The self-cure of frigidity requires determination, patience, and a persistent confidence in self-hypnosis.

Let me suggest that you repeat the following during self-hypnosis:

- I am going to convince myself that I am not really sexually cold or indifferent.
- I am going to remind myself that any negative attitude toward the sex act serves only as a barrier to sexual enjoyment.
- I am going to help my husband improve his lovemaking technique by letting him know about my special needs instead of blaming him for my inability to achieve orgasm.
- I am going to acquire the art of self-relaxation during sexual relations and develop a feeling of abandonment, a willingness to be loved completely.

- I am going to use self-hypnosis and self-analysis to uncover the psychological factors responsible for my
frigidity.
- I am not going to feel guilty or blame myself for my problem in view of all I have learned about the causes of
frigidity.
- Although I may not be responsible for being frigid, I am
responsible if I do nothing about trying to resolve my
problem.
- I am going to get a complete checkup by a gynecologist to
rule out any physical cause of my sexual inadequacy.
- I am going to assure myself, beyond all doubt, that I can
improve my sex life with self-hypnosis.

IMPOTENCE

Impotence in the male is the counterpart of frigidity.

Impotence can be defined as an all-encompassing term
for *sexual inadequacy* in the male. It is not necessarily limited
to a man's inability to get an erection.

There are different types of sexual inadequacy. Some
men are unable to maintain an erection. Others suffer from
a weak semi-erection. Still others suffer from premature or
hasty ejaculation, a sexual disorder that causes wives to be
unsatisfied. Sexual apathy (a lack of desire for sexual relations) is another type of impotence.

In the majority of cases, impotence is caused by psychological factors. It represents the symptom consequence of
unresolved mental conflicts.

Norman's problem was premature ejaculation. His wife
Ruth had never experienced sexual satisfaction since the beginning of their marriage because of her husband's sexual
inadequacy. She was being treated by a laryngologist because
she found it difficult to speak above a whisper. He concluded
following a thorough examination of her throat and vocal
cords that her loss of voice was psychologically induced.

Hypnosis proved the doctor's diagnosis was correct. Ruth talked at considerable length about her sexual frustration in relation to the tension she built up. Norman agreed to be hypnotized and was taught how to use self-hypnosis. He was finally able to develop sufficient staying power to give his wife sexual satisfaction. When the problem of incompatibility was resolved, Ruth's voice returned to normal. It reinforced what I observed in other cases, namely, sexual frustration often produces symptoms in a patient that mask the root cause of the particular health complaint.

SELF-HYPNOTIC SUGGESTIONS

Here are some specific self-hypnotic suggestions to give yourself if your problem is one of sexual inadequacy.

- Practice the technique of inducing self-hypnotic relaxation. Relaxation prior to and during sexual relations improves your staying power and makes the sex act more enjoyable.
- During self-hypnosis try to discover the psychological cause or causes of your impotence.
- Repeat the following during your sessions of self-hypnosis . . . .
- I am not going to use fatigue or the male menopause as an alibi for my inadequacy.
- I am going to eliminate whatever complications are interfering with my inability to function sexually.
- I am going to make every effort to improve my general health, which is bound to influence my sexual vitality.
- I am going to avoid excessive drinking since alcohol in excess may cause me to become impotent.
- I am not going to allow myself to become discouraged, but instead I am going to assure myself that I can ultimately cure myself of my sexual inadequacy with self-hypnosis.

131

SEXUALITY AND AGING

An active sex life can add not only years to your life, but *life* to your years.

Sex-happiness during the later years does not just happen. It is the result of planning and mutual understanding on the part of both husband and wife.

Gerontologists, today, conclude that elderly couples who engage in sexual activity enjoy better health. For example, Dr. Clyde E. Martin, of the Gerontology Research Center at the National Institute of Child Health and Human Development, conducted a survey of 700 older people. He observed that married people who have good sexual relationships with their spouses live longer than single, divorced, or widowed persons.

Couples especially those past sixty, should learn what caresses achieve the richest response, and how to tune these responses so they achieve maximum satisfaction.

If variation in lovemaking banishes monotony and re-kindles a couple's warmth and enthusiasm, it is to be thoroughly recommended for them. Most intelligent people vary their lovemaking enough to keep it out of the humdrum.

Dr. Sallie Schumacher, who heads a sex therapy program and who worked for two years at the Masters and Johnson clinic in St. Louis, Missouri, has this advice:

"Keep enjoying sex as long as you can. Stop feeling ashamed and guilty because you think you're too old for it. Sexual activity can help you keep young. It's a normal function to be enjoyed at any age if one is in reasonably good health."

Although the physical aspects of marriage may taper off as the years pass, there is no reason for not continuing other demonstrations of affection. The warmth, the closeness, and the manifestations of love can be kept alive even during those later years when the sexual act is not always consummated. A kiss, the clasp of hands, a look that betokens the mutual understanding—these are the gestures of affection that should never be abandoned.

I once received a letter from a seventy-five-year-old widower. He had read my book "Helping Yourself With Self-Hypnosis" and wanted to know if he should marry a sixty-five-year-old widow. He described her as congenial—one who hadn't lost her enthusiasm for enjoyable living.

It pleased me to have the opportunity of congratulating him on his never-too-late-for-love attitude and sending him my blessings for a happy wedding.

In a brief note to him, I wrote that love of life is a prerequisite for a happy and enduring love relationship between a husband and wife.

The sex urge continues into your later years. If you are sixty, you still have the capacity to carry on sex relations. There should be no anxiety about it. Enjoy it when you have it. Don't apologize to your wife for lessened frequency. Remember that she is older, too. She wants you to show love for her, but she doesn't expect you to act like a young man of twenty. If one particular time is unsuccessful due to psychological causes, try again. The more you talk about occasional failures, the more you apologize or find excuses, the worse it becomes. Your wife knows that changes are inevitable in you as they are in everyone.

It may be appropriate to state here, even though it may be digressing a bit, that Dr. Levitan, a friend of mine, Professor of Health Education at the University of Maryland, observed "as successful rehabilitation occurs among the aged, so does the will to life—there is a definite interrelationship."

Robert, at the age of sixty-two, began complaining of getting old rapidly. He attributed his premature aging to fatigue. He had never learned to shed the cares and worries of his job. He said he no longer had time for sex because now he was "too tired."

I pointed out to Robert that even the mayor of a large city, or the president of a large firm, despite the tremendous responsibilities of office, has to make time as a husband to continue to have sex with his wife—that one should never be too busy for love.

Robert benefited from learning techniques of self-hypnotism—positive self-suggestion. It transformed him into a new person. He no longer suffered states of anxiety and depression. He resumed his sexual relations with his wife, agreed that he had allowed himself to become a *sexual drop-out*.

Now that he had found himself, so to speak, he was just beginning to live.

Incidentally, Dr. Stanley R. Dean, Professor of psychiatry at the University of Florida and the University of Miami, concluded that physicians should encourage frank discussion about sex between their elderly patients and have them realize that diminished interest in sex is not a signal for abstinence.

Dr. Dean, in addressing the Gerontological Society at their annual meeting, said an interest in sex is not confined to the elderly male, that there was no reason age should be expected to blunt the woman's sexual capacity, performance, or drive.

According to the Center for the Study of Sex Education in Medicine, University of Pennyslvania, "One-tenth of all patients the physician sees in his office have significant *sexual* problems. Half of all couples experience, at one time or another, major sexual maladjustments. The severity of this problem is reflected in the current escalating rate of marriage failures. Sexual problems are among the most sensitive and anguishing that patients bring to their physician."

Remind yourself during self-hypnosis that sex health is indispensable to better physical health and emotional well-being.

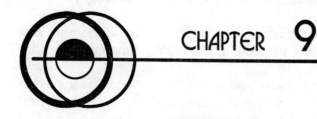

CHAPTER 9

ENDING UNHEALTHY MONEY PROBLEMS THROUGH SELF-HYPNOSIS

VISUALIZE SUCCESS AND PROSPERITY

Thoughts of failure limit your chances to become successful. What you visualize in your mind, you tend to realize in your daily world.

Each day visualize yourself as the person you *want* to become. The mental image comes first, then the subconscious mind goes to work to create the reality. Create a vivid mental picture of yourself as becoming prosperous. The self-image must come before it actually takes place in the outer world. All things begin with this *positive image* or *dream*. Suggest to yourself a feeling of prosperity. See yourself already successful.

Generate self-discipline so that you do not become lazy and unproductive. Without it, you do not accomplish much and you become discontented.

Hypnotically induced self-discipline enables you to take *control* of your life. The great leaders of business and industry became prosperous because they had developed self-discipline.

You cannot fail when you have faith, courage, and persistence. Think prosperity. Think success. Keep away from dispensers of gloom and doom. One of the secrets of successful living is the enjoyment of the moment. This is what life is made of. The present is one moment in time that pauses briefly—and is gone. Use it wisely.

Concentrate on the desire to become prosperous.

If you want to increase your powers of concentration, repeat these suggestions while in your state of self-hypnosis:

* I am going to reduce distractions to a minimum whenever I am reading, studying, or making a major decision.
* I am going to practice becoming a better listener and concentrate on the advice given to me by persons who are already successful and prosperous.
* I am going to become interested in everything I do.

* I am going to make a list of the things I wish to accomplish each day. I am going to use a small pocket notebook for this purpose and carry it with me wherever I go. It will make me more productive and bring me closer to my prosperity goal.

The capacity for success and prosperity lies within all of us. You can get the things out of life you desire—more financial security—better health and happiness, or anything else.

It is a matter of *self-motivation*—unleashing your potential capacities for improved thinking, resulting in a more successful and prosperous way of life.

Success is a *self-taught process*. Develop the *habit* of positive thinking—of surviving disappointments—of converting setbacks into advantages.

Mind power via self-hypnosis can help you achieve success combined with prosperity. Life to a large extent is what you make it. Learn to achieve self-mastery. *Attitude* is very important. New thought patterns become a conditioned reflex. Make successful living and prosperity a *conditioned habit*.

Successful living is a matter of how you use your mind. The power of your mind can enrich your life. You can turn failure into success. Just don't attribute failure to hard luck. Don't tell yourself "I never seem to get the breaks." This is nothing more than alibi-thinking. You make your own breaks.

Successful living has different connotations for different people. To some it means getting what you want, to others it implies being of service to others. It entails making life meaningful—finding success within ourselves, in our overall attitude toward life, and our willingness to work, love, achieve, and become prosperous.

Self-hypnosis can work wonders. It's allowing your mind to become receptive to positive self-given suggestions.

Organization is essential to successful living. It's thinking with a plan. To live without a plan is to sail a ship without a compass. To build, you must be guided by a set of plans. Organize your time. There is a saying "Make what you do today important because you are exchanging a day of your life for it."

Prosperity follows self-confidence. Stop walking backwards. If you do nothing else until you are able to take a step forward, stand still. Self-confidence means the acceptance of responsibilities.

Tony Chance, a young entertainer, asked me to hypnotize him to stop smoking, mainly because it was affecting his singing. He believes in self-hypnosis, is happily married and the father of two beautiful daughters. He lives in Fort Lauderdale, Florida.

He and his band have toured Lake Tahoe, Las Vegas, Atlantic City and Saudi Arabia. He has also planned where he will perform for Americans in 14 different cities.

Tony is an example of someone who has achieved not only the secret of successful living but also prosperity and happiness for himself and his family.

Here is what he had to say about success:

"Overnight success can ruin people. One day they have nothing and the next day they have everything. Sometimes they can't handle it. I already have just about everything I could want. I've taken one step at a time in my career and I'm pleased with the progression so far."

PROSPERITY THROUGH HYPNOSIS

In researching the subject of self-hypnosis and prosperity I came across an article entitled "Making Money With Hypnosis" by Dr. R.V. Shrout. It's a coincidence that I met Dr. Shrout several years ago and had an opportunity to interview him regarding the advantages of having people learn about hypnosis.

Dr. Shrout is the President of the International College for Hypnosis Studies—an educator, author, editor, translator, lecturer, and known internationally for his seminars on hypnosis.

This is what he wrote about prosperity and hypnosis:

"Knowledge is power. We all know that specialized inside information is the key to making more money and enjoying life more. Fortunes have been made in real estate, import-export, stock market, mail order and every kind of business and profession just because someone had inside specialized knowledge.

"Because knowledge is power, it makes sense to get it. That's why the most successful people are willing to get it at any cost.

"You probably know that hypnosis is powerful. Add that fact to what you already know and you come up with a new slogan 'If knowledge is power, and hypnosis is powerful, then the knowledge of hypnosis represents a very great power indeed.' So it makes sense to get whatever you can of this particular kind of inside knowledge."

Dr. Shrout adds:

"To begin with, the first thing to think about is the value of hypnosis. That value can represent money value. It is not only a fascinating study in itself, but a knowledge of the power of suggestion can make you more successful in anything you do—you can motivate yourself by knowing how to program your mind with positive suggestions, taking real command of your own life and destiny. This knowledge alone gives you an inside track in achieving success at anything."

I concur that the above specialized knowledge of hypnosis and self-hypnosis can help you enjoy successful living, together with prosperity unlimited.

CHAPTER **10**

SELF-HYPNOSIS IN COMPETITIVE SPORTS

As I have pointed out self-hypnosis can be utilized successfully in many areas of life. It is not surprising, therefore, to learn that many contestants in sports have taught themselves how to use self-hypnosis to become winners.

We know for a fact that the person who is able to achieve body-mind relaxation performs better than one who is tense and uptight, or one who is over-anxious. Self-relaxation under any circumstances is an *asset*. The golfer, for example who "pyche's" himself with self-confidence, poise, and self-control has better chances of winning in a tournament. There are many golfers who can attest to this. If self-hypnosis works for one athlete, it can work for all others.

With techniques of self-hypnotism, a contestant in sports can acquire greater self-confidence. Self-hypnotism can reduce the incidence of mistakes. One develops better coordination with self-confidence. Mind control influences your performance to advantage. It conquers negativism— the fear of losing. Self-hypnosis increases your power of concentration, enabling you to be less distracted by negative thoughts in performing. It enhances your potential for winning.

Many athletes who have achieved their goals in the sports world have attributed their success to self-hypnotism. They gave themselves positive self-hypnotic suggestions prior to each contest. It was the acceptance of their own suggestions that enabled them to increase their chances of winning.

BREAKING A WORLD RECORD
WITH SELF-HYPNOSIS

James and Jonathan di Donato are the only twins in history who are co-holders of a world record in sports. No other twins in the world have ever presently or previously shared an athletic world record. Their training, as in their record setting (both requiring incredible discipline), is done side-by-side in parallel twin fashion.

The "Tiger Twins" (as they are referred to by the press) just prior to their big swim here in Florida, contacted me asking me to hypnotize them the day before their attempt to swim 20 miles from Fort Lauderdale to Pompano Beach, Florida. They hoped that with techniques of self-hypnotism, they would be able to set another world record.

I hypnotized James and Jonathan separately. They proved excellent subjects.

It was gratifying to learn that they applied self-hypnotic suggestions all during their swimming and achieved their goal, swimming farther than they had in previous attempts to swim the English Channel, thus breaking another world record.

I felt our readers might like to share what James had to write regarding their unique experience.

"My twin brother Jonathan and I contacted Dr. Caprio before our attempt to reset the swimming record for "Marathon Butterfly." We previously had set three world distance records. We wanted desperately to prove, especially to ourselves, that we could attain our goal. The previous summer of 1981 we had our greatest setback. We aborted our English Channel attempt after only one hour and nine minutes. So this upcoming swim was different. The carefree confidence, the mental paradise of early swims was lacking. We were carrying a tremendous weight on our shoulders. I was engulfed in great fear of incapability. All the hopes and positiveness of the past seemed unreachably far away. Heavy dread dominated my mind. I was obsessed with the seemingly inevitable feeling of terrific pain. I could not get the "I give up" feeling out of my head.

"I had heart palpitations for weeks leading up to the swim, originally set for late April, thinking it was due to physical stress.

"Almost as if it were by fate, we met Dr. Caprio who had been practicing and teaching hypnosis and self-hypnosis for many years. He welcomed us warmly. He himself exudes self-relaxation. Fortunately for me, it was contagious. As a result I soon became a little less anxious. We discussed my swimming and my goals so that he would have a knowledge about the important things on my mind. Then, through a method of visually induced drowsiness and physical relaxation, he had each of us in the hypnotic state. He hypnotized us separately.

"While I was in this dream-like, relaxed state, he emphasized the importance of self-relaxation. He told me not to worry and encouraged me to do my best. He reassured me I would set a new world record, that I *can*, I *must* and I *will* "go the distance." That following week for the first time in two months, I didn't have any heart palpitations. Each night in bed, before falling asleep, I would, in my relaxed state, repeat Dr. Caprio's positive hypnotic suggestions.

"I'd like to add that after my session of hypnosis, I was surprised to find that my brother Jonathan and I had been practicing a form of self-hypnosis for several years and we weren't even aware of it.

"To prepare our marathon swim we would consciously plant a seed of confidence and determination in our minds through the repetition of positive thoughts. We had (still have) a two-page list of thoughts which are inspirational to us. We referred to the list daily and in each workout, we would focus in on one or two of those ideas. This had helped us many times in the darker moments of our long swims.

"Dr. Caprio, however, was vital. Our swims were not getting any easier. He showed us a much clearer and more efficient method of enforcing positive ideas—the method whereby one exercises self-motivation and self-given suggestions while in the hypnotic state. Dr. Caprio made us aware of the great importance of self-hypnotically induced body-mind relaxation.

"In conclusion, we made it. We went the distance 16.5 miles—a new world distance record for swimming using the butterfly stroke. The total time was nearly 14 hours. Nine of those hours we swam in darkness against seemingly impossible conditions. We had a strong current running against us and we plowed into 3 to 5 foot waves which constantly bombarded our faces, chests, and arms and made breathing a tremendous challenge.

"The conditions were far worse than we'd ever anticipated. We had the type of seas that would normally have had us exhausted within the first hour.

"How did we do it? It was hypnosis and self-hypnosis, thanks to Dr. Caprio, that made it possible."

(Signed) James di Donato.

Regarding the details of their unusual experience, the *Fort Lauderdale Sun Sentinel* published the following:

> Twin brothers from Fort Lauderdale, swimming all night, broke the world distance record for the butterfly stroke Thursday.
>
> Jonathan and James di Donato, 28-year-old swimming instructors, swam 16-½ miles from Fort Lauderdale to Pompano and back in just under 14 hours. The previous record was 15 miles. "The weather was a monster," said Jonathan. "The easiest way to explain is that the weather was a nightmare. It was pitch-black. We had hoped to go 20 miles but the water was too bad. The current was so bad this morning we swam only two-fifths of a mile for the last hour," he said. "Coming back they were swimming through an awful current," said a witness, Bud Stafford, who manned one of the three boats that accompanied the brothers. At dawn the wind picked up and they were swimming into waves. James collapsed in the sand along the beach when he finished, and was treated by emergency medical personnel. Jonathan blacked out 15 minutes later. The di Donato brothers began their swim shortly after 7 P.M. Thursday. They each swam behind small boats with outboard motors, and were allowed to eat four minutes each hour while dog-paddling. "While you're treading water you have to eat the whole time, just so you won't die," Jonathan said.

The di Donato brothers are already in the Guinness Book of the World Records for swimming the Butterfly stroke for 10 miles. Their hope is to swim the 20-mile stretch of the English Channel with that stroke.

The di Donato twins, the only swimmers to succeed using the Butterfly stroke in a long-distance swim, achieved still another world record. On August 21, 1983, they were the first to swim the 28.5 miles around Manhattan Island using the most strenuous stroke, the Butterfly.

The 29-year-old Fort Lauderdale swim instructors are the only twins to co-hold a world record in sports.

Incidentally, this side-by-side swim around Manhattan benefited the Center for the Study of Multiple Births and Week of the Ocean (Both are national non-profit organizations dedicated to research.)

Their swimming feats have led to appearances on the Phil Donahue Show, Good Morning America, P.M. Magazine and the Today Show, to coverage in *People Magazine, Swimming World Magazine, Vegetarian Times, The Wall Street Journal, The New York Times,* and the *International Herald Tribune.* The twins have also appeared as winners in *Cosmopolitan* magazine's first Male Centerfold Contest (June 1982, p. 226). The identical twin bachelors were among the 10 finalists selected from a field of 7,000 contestants.

Just prior to their swim around Manhattan, James and Jonathan contacted me once again about wanting to be hypnotized.

I hypnotized them prior to August 7th, 1983, when they left Fort Lauderdale for New York for the final segment of their demanding training.

Their swim began at 96th St.—Hell Gate—at the East River at 9:36 A.M., Sunday morning, August 21, 1983, low tide, full moon. They swam counterclockwise around Manhattan Island and arrived at their destination (the finish, 96th St.) nine hours later at 6:36 P.M.

It is interesting that the Butterfly method of swimming, although apparently as graceful as a dolphin's swimming, is also known for its punishing difficulty. The swimmer must pull his upper body and arms out of the water on each stroke and maintain a two-beat dolphin kick (the legs remain together like a fin, whipping up and down twice for each arm stroke).

The twins hold a triple world record. Manhattan has never been swum successfully side-by-side by any two swimmers. It has never been swum by twins nor has the Butterfly stroke been swum 28 miles.

A sports authority claimed that the "Tiger Twins" are on the threshold of being "the greatest athletes on earth," and "the most famous twins in the world."

I feel flattered for having been chosen to hypnotize each of them with the gratification that their use of self-hypnosis enabled them to achieve their goal.

The 29-year-olds, who tried unsuccessfully to swim the English Channel in 1981, are the first twins to swim around Manhattan Butterfly style simultaneously.

Said James: "We love New York. We lived there the first 17 years of our life—and as Frank Sinatra said in the song, 'If you can make it there, you can make it anywhere.'"

Incidentally, they are planning to swim the 21-mile, more torturous English Channel in the summer of 1984.

Jonathan commented "We have stress days on Monday, Wednesday, and Friday when we swim two to five miles against the current with one-pound weights on our wrists. We also do push-ups, and hand stands, sit-ups—you name it."

Their claim to the Hall of Fame is well deserved. My personal congratulations to them for their faith in self-hypnotism.

By the way, Forbes Carlile, Australia's leading swimming coach, reported how he has helped several swimmers to Olympic Championships with hypnosis.

Someone asked me "Can hypnosis improve my tennis game?"

My answer was yes. Hypnotic conditioning can overcome faults in your game and reduce tension. The application of self-hypnosis instills confidence which is paramount in any sport.

Positive auto-suggestion in one form or another has

been used by athletes before with excellent results, through the elimination of the fear of failure.

The great Knute Rockne hypnotized his team between halves, especially when they were losing. His personal magnetism and his exhortations had such a powerful hypnotic effect that the team went out and literally swarmed over the opposition.

If you expect to lose, you will lose.

The subconscious mind accepts the thought—thoughts you give it. Self-hypnosis enables you to eliminate negative thoughts—thoughts that block you from winning. Self-hypnotism helps you to recondition your subconscious mind to the *will to win*. Self-confidence is essential to becoming a *winner* not only in competitive sports, but in all areas of life.

SELF-HYPNOTIC AUTOSUGGESTIONS
ATHLETES CAN GIVE THEMSELVES
TO IMPROVE THEIR SKILLS

It has been an established fact that Mind Power and Mind-Control can influence the performance of professional athletes in competitive sports of any kind (golf, tennis, swimming, running, bowling, Olympic events, boxing, etc.)

To cite an example, Muhammad Ali was known to have "psyched" himself before going into the ring—that he was unbeatable—that he was the greatest fighter in the world.

Here are some specific self-given suggestions recommended for athletes.

* I am going to use self-hypnosis as many times as necessary so that I can apply to advantage the knowledge I have gained.
* I have the power within me to control and influence my mind at will—I can quickly convert negative thinking into positive thinking—eliminate fear thoughts and replace them with success thoughts.

* I am going to develop a *relaxed attitude* prior to and during my performance in a competitive contest.
* I am going to make good use of self-hypnotism to inspire sustaining confidence in myself.
* I am going to remind myself not to become *over-anxious* and *tense*.
* I am going to write on a card a list of specific positive attitudes that I am going to adopt and label them *self-hypnosis reminders*. I am going to carry the card with me in my wallet or purse as I would my driver's license and refer to it daily. It will condition my mind to a *will to win*.
* Self-hypnosis can help me develop the kind of poise and relaxation that will enhance my ability to do my best.
* I am going to tell myself—this is going to be a good day for me—that I am going to experience an inner feeling of self-confidence—that I am capable of performing better than I ever have before.
* I am going to apply self-hypnosis as often as necessary until I achieve a maximum feeling of *self-mastery*.
* I am convinced that a *positive image* of myself will increase my chances of winning.
* I refuse to allow myself to become emotionally upset by noises from spectators.
* Instead of feeling uptight, I am going to remind myself *relax and enjoy*.
* I am going to regard self-hypnosis as a supplementary method of improving my *potential* as an athlete.
* I am going to use positive self-communication on rising in the morning and on going to bed.
* Mind-Control and Self-Relaxation can alleviate fear and tension.
* For inspiration, I am going to visualize the trophies I have won in the past.
* I am going to improve my power of concentration and think only of winning.
* I am determined to make *winning a reality* instead of a *dream*.

One particular person—a professional runner, informed me that he combined self-hypnosis with *visual imagery* which proved successful. For example, he visualized himself as crossing the finish line well in front of everyone else, not even breathing hard, while his exhausted opponents straggled in behind.

Some athletes claimed that the power of prayer was a deciding factor in winning.

Discover for yourself what works best for you. There is abundant evidence, nevertheless, that positive self-communication in any form is the *key* to becoming a *winner* in your chosen competitive sport.

CHAPTER **11**

MAKING YOUR GOLDEN YEARS MEANINGFUL AND ENJOYABLE

Your later years can be the most glamorous and happiest years of your life. Positive self-hypnotic communication can help you overcome imaginary ills, complacency, and lethargy for a full life.

Remind yourself no one is born with negative thoughts. They do not originate from a germ or virus. They are self-induced. By the same token, no one is born with positive thoughts. They too are *self-induced*. The transition from negative to positive lies in the power of self-*hypnosis*.

Realize now that you have abundant time for leisure activities and reflections.

Growing old is a matter of *attitude* not arteries. You may age physically but you need not grow old mentally.

With self-hypnosis you can change your way of thinking, your mode of living, and acquire sufficient knowledge, self-understanding, and wisdom to achieve the special goals you set for yourself.

If you want to stay young, keep well, and live longer, here are some anti-aging suggestions to give yourself—

* I have a right to survive—to add years to my life—to enjoy life. I have a right to be happy.
* I decided never to despair. I realize that life is a battlefield. It's a fight to the finish. But with courage and patience I can come out on top despite the worst circumstances. Darwin was right when he said life is the survival of the fittest. The weak succumb, the strong survive. Each of us makes his choice. We can survive or perish.
* I am capable of developing self-motivation—the motivation to want to put life into my years and not merely years into my life.
* I choose to enhance the quality of my life—to adopt a healthier lifestyle—to live life to its fullest—making life meaningful and enjoyable.
* I am never too old to acquire a new lease on life, to learn, to keep active, to think positive thoughts, to laugh, and be of service to others.

* I am going to remain young in mind and heart by finding new pleasures, new interests, new friends.
* I have a gladness to be alive, a will to live, and this will keep me forever young.
* I am as old as I feel. Growing old is a matter of attitude.
* I will never become bored as long as I develop enthusiasm in everything I do.
* I am going to replace negative thinking with positive and optimistic thoughts.

Louise (my wife) and I had the good fortune of meeting a charming woman in the course of our travels to the Scandinavian countries and once again on a Mediterranean cruise. Our friend Mamie Clayton, a very remarkable woman, is presently in her nineties.

When I asked her what she thought about growing old, she replied: "I remind myself that my life has been one of thankful living, each day finding more and more to be thankful for. I believe all things work out for the good. I consider I am one of the most lucky people living. I have so much to be grateful for."

One of the reasons for Mamie's longevity, no doubt, is her anti-aging attitude toward life.

What is your own philosophy of life? Did you ever formulate one? Everyone needs to put down on paper what he believes about everything—life, people, religion, etc. You may discover much about yourself.

A positive philosophy incorporates the idea of a purpose to living, a faith in a Higher Power, greater than man, an appreciation of the wonders of the universe, a joy of life. It fosters human understanding, growth of personality, unselfishness, and serenity through freedom from guilt, fear, anxiety, and hate. It acknowledges the imperfections and frailties of human nature, enables us to develop a realistic understanding of their origin, and inspires a desire for a more positive lifestyle.

A meaningful way of life—healthier, happier, and more enjoyable is yours if you are willing to make the necessary effort. Forget yesterday. *Live today.* Make self-improvement a life-lasting habit.

Goethe, the philosopher, inferred that living is an art which everyone must learn but no one can teach. Although I've admired his writings, I do not concur that the only way one can acquire wisdom is through personal experiences. I believe the art of successful living can be taught.

Incidentally, I would like to share with you a legacy I inherited from my father. He did not have a formal education but was a *self-taught philosopher.*

Here are some things he passed on to me:

Keep your life simplified. Accept certain basic truths, certain fundamental common sense rules and utilize them to advantage. Knowledge becomes wisdom only after it has been put to practical use.

Make self-improvement a lifetime habit. Convince yourself that you have the ability to control and influence your thinking. Convert negative thoughts into positive ones. Inspire your life with achievements. Happiness comes from the joy of accomplishments, from knowing that you are improving every day in every way. Be an avid reader. Never stop learning.

Make wisdom a priority. Don't become a casualty of health dissipations. Develop health intelligence. Build a sound body and a sound mind. Examine your living habits. The lifestyle you choose determines your physical and mental well-being. When you enjoy good health you are more apt to be happy, and if you're happy, you are most likely to succeed.

Success depends on the kind of planning you do. Jot plans down on paper and if they don't work out, then what? Make new plans to fit your altered circumstances. Nothing should be so inflexible that it prevents making new plans for a changed situation.

Successful living is both a science and an art. Science has been defined as "organized facts." The science of intelligent living can be defined as the application of organized plans that deal with the style of life—a system or technique of living conducive to better health.

Be all you can. My family motto has always been *Labor et amor omnia vincit* (Work and love conquer all things). It was inscribed on a plaque in my library.

If you develop enthusiasm in your chosen life career, you are less likely to be bored.

Success in life is not a matter of acquiring wealth. It implies keeping out of debt, achieving a degree of financial security. There is no need for an obsessional drive for money, but you do need to be practical enough to know money is important to survival. You can't simply be a dreamer. You must work for what you desire in life. Success and happiness must be earned.

Analyze each problem as it comes along. All of us have problems, but there are solutions to them. Study the facts— the right answers will emerge. It may be possible that you are the problem. If so, subject yourself to a self-examination. Analyze your liabilities. It is only common sense that if you can't get along with yourself, you will have difficulty getting along with others.

Don't ever be discouraged. Despair brings on depression and this in turn affects those around you. It's not so much what happens to you, but how you react to it that's important.

Develop the perseverance and determination to get ahead. Assure yourself that nothing in the world can keep you down. Don't join the ranks of the dead beats—persons who are unhappy because of never having achieved anything worthwhile through their own efforts.

Success is everything—but not without love. Love is an active verb. To say you love someone is not enough. Love must be proof of love. It was my parents who taught me the meaning of love. It was their legacy to me. Love is sharing the beauty and ecstasies of life; the common denominator of all aspects of life itself. It is the parent of all other forms of love. It is the great trunk which has many branches, all nourished by the same roots—love to endure, to tolerate, to help others. To understand life, you must first understand the nature of love. Never be too busy to love.

Devote your energies to being kind to others. Kindness has its own reward. Buddha must have known this for he said; "To do a little good is more than to accomplish great conquests." Kindness means doing things for other people. It's the art of being unselfish. Life is too short not to be kind. My father was a kind man. He taught me not to harbor malice toward anyone.

Learn to enjoy life. You have earned the right. Go after what you want in life, but after you get it enjoy it. Make living easier for yourself. Laugh a bit every day. Laughter is the music of the soul. Don't take yourself too seriously.

Live an everyday religion based on ethical precepts. Develop a seven-day week religion based on ethics, a religion founded on the Golden Rule—treating your fellowman as you would want to be treated.

Don't hold grudges or hate anyone. Judge your fellow man not by his race, religion, or bank account, but by the quality of his character.

Will Durant, at the age of 92, left this advice for posterity. "My final lesson of 2000 years of history is: Love one another. Love is the most practical thing in the world. If you take an attitude of love, you'll get along."

If you want your life to be meaningful make a careful survey of what you want in life. Let *self*-hypnosis help you achieve what you desire.

To enjoy life more, you must *plan* to enjoy it. I recommend that you get a copy of *How To Enjoy Yourself* by Perry Wilbur (Prentice-Hall). It reveals everything you need to know to help you lead a richer, healthier, and happier lifestyle—today, tomorrow, and every day of your life.

The publisher describes it as "The antidote book to un-

happiness and depression. It includes hundreds of ideas to make life more fun, more enjoyable—every day of the year."
Here are some capsule excerpts:

- Love of oneself and love of life itself are the best antidotes for unhappiness.

- Every day should be a new passion for living—a new day to enjoy the fruits that you so richly deserve—a new day to learn and accomplish what you set out to do.

- You can generate a determined resolution to live today, and every day with a positive attitude toward yourself and life.

- Self-happiness is indispensable to enjoying life.

- The capacity to make life happier stems from the conviction that happiness is self-created and can be cultivated.

- If you want to attain happiness, start with yourself. You cannot expect people to change or the world to change to suit your needs and desires. You yourself must change.

My wife and I had the pleasure of knowing Fred Fassen, Past President of the American Association of Retired Persons (AARP) and his wife Grace. He was generous enough to describe for me his ideas about retirement.

"Retirement is not a withdrawal from life. Properly planned and properly prepared for it can be the most active and most productive period of an individual's life. Nor is retirement a necessary period of rest. You don't need more rest the day after you are sixty-five than the day before—what you need is a new channel for your activities now.

"The most important goal of our retirement should be meaningful use of time—whatever time is given to us.

"Retirement can be the most rewarding and the richest time of an individual's life. It can mean involvement in politics, adult education, travel and community activities or it can mean sitting on a park bench waiting for another game of shuffleboard. The choice is ours. There is nothing wrong with shuffleboard, or fishing, or just sitting in the sun. There are leisure activities that we have earned the right to enjoy. But they must be only one part of retirement life—they must not deter us from activities with a deeper meaning, pursuits through which we can obtain the true satisfaction of being needed, of being useful, of being involved or contributing something to our society and to our fellow man.

"The greatest percentage of ailments of aging are caused not by physical but rather by mental deterioration. When we keep ourselves mentally alert and active, we haven't time to deteriorate. When we remain totally involved in the world around us, we are too busy for self-pity. When we are concerned with society's problems, we have no time to dwell on our own.

"In the final analysis, it is up to you to determine the importance of your life in retirement. To decide whether you will retire to the rocking chair or whether you will continue to serve and not be served as long as you live."

In the words of Julia Ward, "Never fear old age: The sugar of life is at the bottom of the cup."

COPING WITH LONELINESS

Loneliness has reached epidemic proportions in the United States. It is a major cause of sickness, mental illness, alcoholism, and drug addiction.

Would it amaze you to learn that one person out of ten hasn't a single friend—that women are the lonelier sex—that there are about 14 million unattached women, twice the number of single men over thirty?

Is loneliness self-curable? Yes. You can beat loneliness and enjoy a new life—you can escape from the dark pit of loneliness that entraps millions of people, but you've got to work at it—to help yourself, as it were.

The shy teenager who cannot get a date—the divorcee with young children to support who longs for adult companionship—the widow who spends her time visiting her late husband's grave—the elderly man in a nursing home waiting for death.

All these are classic cases of people whose lives are haunted by loneliness—and in every case the cure for their problem lies within themselves.

Loneliness is self-created—sugar-coated self-pity—a symptom not a condition per se. Anyone can feel lonely—married or unmarried, alone or in a crowd.

It is not uncommon for many men and women who confess to being lonely, to feel bitter and unhappy. They generally have a defeatist attitude toward life. Some widows, due to their feelings of self-pity, believe they do not fit in with groups of married people.

Dr. Helena Lopata, Director of The Center for Comparative Study of Social Roles at Loyola University, Chicago, and the author of "Widowhood In An American City," claims that loneliness in widowhood is not just the result of a woman's grieving over the death of her husband. She has observed that there are various reasons why some widows are lonely—"One problem is that a widow's friends fail to understand what she's going through after her husband dies. They think she's being too emotional for too long, so they start to desert her. Then the widow begins sanctifying her husband, imagining him as much better than he actually was. This irritates her grown children as well as her friends, and they are further encouraged to leave her alone, adding to her loneliness."

Dr. Lopata cites reasons why some widows prefer not to remarry—they like being independent, and they may not want to go through the trouble of adjusting to someone else again.

Nevertheless, it is hard for anyone to be really lonely in the true sense of the word. If they feel lonely, it is because they are emotionally withdrawn from other people by choice or by a lack of knowledge of how to draw others to them or how to reach out and turn an acquaintance or a stranger into a friend.

Lila had been referred to me for counseling because of loneliness. Her doctor informed me that she was in good health. When I saw her she told me about being unable to adjust emotionally following the death of her husband. She claimed she felt only half-alive and that she would never be happy again.

I explained to Lila, to be unhappy temporarily under such circumstances was normal, but to remain unhappy was unhealthy.

There are countless numbers of widows like Lila who allow themselves to become casualties of loneliness and unhappiness. They hug their grief to their breasts for fear they will forget. They keep reminding themselves of their sorrow, verbalizing their unhappiness.

Lila agreed to being hypnotized. When she realized she was afraid to be happy, subconsciously reluctant to enjoy herself, she began to acquire a new lease on life.

Even though she had the advantage of being financially secure, emotionally she was insecure and had lost her sense of self-esteem. It was necessary for her to understand that a healthy love of oneself is a prerequisite to a love of life.

Lila was taught the technique of self-hypnotism. She decided to develop a more positive image of herself. Her insight enabled her to conquer her feelings of self-pity. Positive self-communication via self-hypnosis became her antidote for loneliness.

Incidentally, women have by far the greater problem if they are unattached. The problem for many women is that they do not wish to seem aggressive, so they sit down pining for an aggressive male to come into their lives. Many have children and cannot go out frequently and be available to meet men.

Because there are more available women than men— less than 7 million men, widowers, divorced, separated, or bachelors, compared to 14 million unattached women— there is a change in the marriage market that women must adjust to in this modern world.

No woman of any age need fear that she will be left by the wayside all alone and lonely if she is friendly, pleasant, and outgoing. For every woman who marries a man older than herself, there is a woman who marries a man considerably younger. A surprising number of men tell me they are in love with older women.

Remember, if you are a bitter, supercritical person, people will fear and avoid you. But if you radiate warmth and understanding, people will be drawn to your side. Everyone seeks to be appreciated and understood. You will never be lonely if you show people that you care about them.

The loneliest people in the world are those who concentrate only on themselves. As soon as you are interested in other people and other things, you will not be thinking about yourself. It is impossible to be lonely when you are not thinking about yourself—to say, "I am alone, I am lonely." Only when you start to feel sorry for yourself can you feel loneliness.

Did you know that Joan Crawford's greatest hangup was her inability to combat loneliness, the seeds of which were planted in her childhood? Her parents had separated before she was born. Her fatherless childhood added to her stressful sense of insecurity, for which she over-compensated by becoming over-ambitious. Success became a compulsion—an obsession. Career success was was more important to her than marriage happiness. She achieved stardom at the expense of three marriages.

Joan blamed no one but herself for her unhappy marital experiences, as evidenced by her statements:

"Maybe I was the one who gave myself three unhappy endings and untold loneliness. I'm the sum of everything that's ever happened to me, every mistake. I've made every tear I have ever shed."

It is more than a coincidence that women whose parents were divorced bring on their own marriage-failures. This is not to imply that unhappiness is inherited, but divorces often pass from one generation to another.

In Joan's case, parental incompatibility and unhappiness were no asset to her. It influenced her more than she was aware of. It became an emotional scar, never to be forgotten.

Joan apparently was lonely most of her life. She tried in later years to overcome her feelings of aloneness by making every effort to gain attention.

Without a doubt she was extremely talented—a born actress. It gave her an opportunity to communicate with the world.

Her frivolity and laughter at parties or on special occasions camouflaged her deep-seated unhappiness. Loneliness became her hang-up—her nemesis.

When interviewed, following the death of her last husband, Alfred Steele, she readily admitted she was very lonely. This is understandable—a stress reaction experienced by many widows.

What a tragedy that Joan found loneliness so stressful. It became her downfall and certainly contributed indirectly, if not directly, to her death. Little did she realize that loneliness is self-curable.

Nonetheless, here are some positive self-given suggestions that will help you conquer loneliness. Repeat them to yourself or out loud during your sessions of self-hypnosis as often as you find necessary.

* I am going to stop thinking about myself, my own wants and needs, and start thinking of others.
* I am going to establish meaningful relationships with new friends.
* I am going to tell myself every day that I have a lot to give to society. I refuse to lead a wasted life.
* I am not going to fear rejection.
* I know that I can take up new interests, hobbies, church activities, or community work that will keep me from becoming preoccupied with problems, feelings, and emotions.
* I can take up volunteer work in a hospital or a school, two or three days a week.

* I am going to keep physically and mentally active. I can try golf, tennis, or shuffleboard or do crossword puzzles or play Scrabble.
* I am going to stay abreast of new books and current events that will help me engage in stimulating conversations.
* I am going to make the first move to form new friendships, relationships, or romances.
* I am going to remind myself that there are many other lonely people who are coping with loneliness successfully.
* I am going to learn how to enjoy my aloneness time and that it's no stigma to be alone.

The rewards for overcoming loneliness are great, but until you conquer it, loneliness is something you will carry with you wherever you go. However, once you lose it, you will be free to relax, to quit running away from yourself, to be happy, to feel at ease. It cannot catch up with you ever again, even on a desert island.

Dr. Garland Fross, world-famous hypnotist, whom I had known over the years told me: "Anyone can attain true peace of mind, optimism, courage, will power, and energy by silently talking to himself."

He recommends that you do not let negative thoughts steal into your mind like thieves in the night claiming that they will rob you of your greatest treasures. He suggests that you bar the door to all negative thoughts—that you post a mental sentry with the challenge—"None but the good and positive thoughts will enter here." In this way your life can become positive instead of negative.

Communicate with yourself in positive and optimistic terms. You are what your subconscious accepts as a fact. If you tell yourself that you will have greater confidence and self-control and believe what you tell yourself, it will come to pass.

Convince yourself that positive self-communication during self-hypnosis can help you enjoy *better health*. It is the most effective way of talking to yourself. Relaxing your mind and body and repeating out loud the positive suggestions you desire is the easiest and most efficient way of communication with yourself. It might be interesting to realize that one suggestion given during self-hypnosis is equivalent to having received the same suggestion 40 times in the so-called waking state.

Each of us knows better than anyone else what we need to tell ourselves. To make the self-given suggestions more effective, you should write them down, then condense them into short phrases. They should be *permissive, positive* and *encouraging,* and not repressive, prohibitory, or negative.

* I am becoming happier every day.
* My cheerfulness is increasing by leaps and bounds.
* I am becoming more pleasant and agreeable all the time.
* I am attaining true peace of mind.
* I am making my dreams (goals) become realities.
* Positive thinking is rapidly becoming my way of life.
* I am communicating better every day.
* I am developing more energy and vitality every day.
* I am concentrating better every day.
* I am becoming more outgoing every day.

The above are just sample-suggestions you can give yourself.

Richard Harding, age 85, consulted me here in Fort Lauderdale regarding insomnia, fatigue, and depression. He had known me while I was in the private practice of psychiatry in Washington, D.C. Richard decided to move to Florida for health reasons. However, he became unhappy and depressed thinking he should have remained in Washinton where his friends were. Nevertheless, I decided to have "Dick" as he preferred to be called, examined by a physician who practiced gerontology (illnesses of the elderly). The physician discovered that Dick had a chronic heart condition, that his blood pressure was elevated and told him he was "a very sick man." When he heard this he became more depressed. He became obsessed with the idea that he didn't have too long to live. The physician gave him his medication and suggested that he return for another checkup. Dick decided not to return and instead asked me if I thought hypnosis would help him get over his depression.

I gave him two sessions of hypnosis and on his third visit taught him the technique of self-hypnosis.

Prior to becoming ill he had gone into the ocean for his daily swim.

Following three sessions of hypnotherapy, he became an entirely different individual. He began to enjoy eating, which he had not done, slept better and changed his attitude toward life. He told me "I'm not ready to die. I am going to live to be 95. My trouble is that I'm worrying about dying, and I have a lot to be grateful for.

"I refuse to cash in my chips." Much to my surprise, he made a miraculous recovery from his depression. He attributed it to *self-hypnosis*—the repetition of positive self-given suggestions.

Dick is looking forward to his 86th birthday and goes to the ocean every day, weather permitting. He walks a mile every day along the beach—eats at nice restaurants once a week, has made many new friends, has redecorated his apartment, and is as cheerful and alert as any human can be.

His case demonstrated what a changed attitude can do even for someone his age.

GROW WISER—NOT OLDER

There is only one way to avoid aging. Each senior citizen must realize that he was given a longer lifespan for a purpose and that purpose calls for normal living, fulfilling his talents and capacities, and radiating the love and wisdom that the years have brought him. Thus, he can live it up and grow and not just grow old.

Tell yourself that you are growing wiser—not older. You definitely can learn through self-hypnosis to stay young longer and enjoy happier living.

Bernard E. Nash, executive director of the American Association of Retired Persons, reports that there exists an international movement for the aging. He informs us that in London last fall representatives of 17 organizations from 13 nations approved the establishment of an International Federation on Aging—a worldwide movement to promote the status and well-being of older persons.

Bernard Nash was elected President of IFA at the London organizational meeting. He believes that the IFA will serve as an instrument for improving the quality of life for the elderly throughout the world.

KNOW WHAT YOU WANT OUT OF LIFE

Positive self-given suggestions can enable you to plan for a new way of life. Many of us are afraid to make plans out of fear that they will never materialize.

When elderly couples tell me, "Doctor, how can you be certain of the future? Suppose something should happen? What then? Isn't it better to live for the present so that you will never be disappointed?"

My reply is, "If your plan of life, in accordance with your individual desires should suddenly be blocked, simply make *new* plans to fit your altered circumstances."

No plan should be too inflexible to prevent making new plans to meet a situation.

During self-hypnotism keep the following in mind:

- Do not neglect your personal appearance. Observe personal hygiene. Look your best. Take pride in the way you dress.
- Keep yourself active. Never stop learning. Avoid idleness. Never allow yourself to become discouraged.
- Make the most of your assets and talents. Gain self-confidence through accomplishments.

- Enjoy life. Get your weekly quota of entertainment. Cultivate new interests. Travel if you like. Enjoy your friends. Read good books. Listen to good music. Have fun.

- Take an inventory of yourself. It's never too late to change for the better. Analyze your shortcomings and correct them. Become the kind of person you prefer to be. Avoid prejudices, religious or racial. Harbor malice toward no one. Don't become your own enemy. Be glad you are alive. Change your way of thinking.

- Make yourself useful. Be sociable. Share with others what you have learned through experience. Lend your cooperation to worthy causes. Help those in despair. Assume life's responsibilities willingly. Do your best in everything you do. And last but not least, develop a positive anti-aging philosophy of life.

Incidentally, the lifespan of people is increasing beyond the Biblical age of threescore and ten. This is attributable to medical progress.

Dr. Adolph Abraham Apton, author of *Your Mind And Appearance,* predicts that the normal human lifespan will definitely increase in the future and that an age of one hundred will not be uncommon.

He informs us: "With an almost universal knowledge of the laws of hygiene, avoidance of excess, balanced diet, sufficient sleep, and a regular physical examination—with all its clinical information at the disposal of the race—a great deal is done to prevent a so-called run-down condition from developing further unless a person is unbearably harassed economically or given to various addictions."

Regarding our present lifespan, men can expect to live an average age of 79 and women to 82. The national life expectancy for men aged 65 is 77 years; for women it is 81 years.

We have reason to be encouraged regarding this

lifespan. Dr. Joseph P. Harchovec of the University of Southern California's Gerontological Center claims that anyone can live to be one hundred years even if his parents or grandparents died at an early age. He attributed premature deaths in many instances to improper eating, exercising too little, and not being able to relax. He recommends the following for those who wish to live longer.

1. Avoid eating large meals, going too long between meals, irregular eating habits, and food that is sweetened with sugar. Overeating brings on diabetes, high blood pressure, heart disease, and dozens of other less obvious but killing disease.

2. Get plenty of exercise. If you want to keep your body in good health, you must use it. Proper exercise is the closest thing to an anti-aging pill now available. And the exercise should be intense enough to bring on panting of the heart to receive any benefit from it.

3. Learn to control emotional and outside pressures. They cause or contribute to such chronic diseases as arteriosclerosis, coronary heart disease, and hypertension. People with high blood pressure, for instance, suffer twice as many heart attacks as people with normal blood pressure.

"Every person," according to Dr. Harchovec, "has a limit to the amount of physical endurance, mental concentration, and emotional strain he can safely handle without overextending his capacities. With careful training these limits can be extended, but the strategy for long life is to use yourself to these limits without exceeding them. No one should drive himself to the point of a breakdown. We must learn to respect the built-in warning systems in our bodies and listen when they tell us 'we're exceeding our capacities.'"

Dr. Harchovec contends that anyone can stretch his lifespan like a rubber band, no matter what his (or her) present age might be.

Dr. Alexander Leaf of Massachusetts General Hospital and Harvard Medical School, who became interested in a scientific investigation of longevity and the aging process, had an opportunity to visit three so-called Shangri-Las—

Ecuador, Kashmir and Russia. Dr. Leaf believes that some people may age faster than others because in some instances disease processes are the result of environmental factors and others may be built into the genes themselves. He also observed that men die earlier than women at a rate of almost two to one. Some claim this is so because men are exposed to greater hazards.

Stress apparently shortens life. People who retire and feel they no longer have anything to contribute to society and are no longer useful, die sooner than those who are active.

Although it is a common notion that our life expectancy is threescore and ten, Dr. Leaf claims there is no biological limit that says that 70 years is all the human body can live in comfort and vigorous health. He believes the human body can function effectively until one hundred.

What did Dr. Leaf learn from the centenarians he studied around the world? Did he find anything in common among them? Here is what he reports:

The common factor seems to be a continued active life with a great deal of physical activity. Psychological factors also seemed to be important. In none of these areas do the old people ever retire. They continue to be socially useful and to live with their families. They are highly esteemed for their age and wisdom. They seem to be people with a very *positive* outlook, an optimistic view that things are always getting better. When things don't seem to be so good, they say they don't worry because they can't change things anyway.

It appears that the people Dr. Leaf refers to have mastered the art of adding years to their life and life to their years with *Mind Power*. They apparently discovered the wisdom of adopting a positive and optimistic outlook on life which can be achieved, incidentally, with *self-hypnosis*.

Dr. R. F. Mines, Dean of Research, Miami-Dade Community College, Florida, advocated *activity* as a requirement for longevity. He claims that to achieve peace of mind you have to work at it, but the effort is worth it. He has found in his research studies that the more one engages in constructive activity the less dissatisfied he is with himself. He informs us that it is one of the best ways to achieve a positive outlook, both toward the world and your own being.

SALIENT POINTS TO KEEP IN MIND

1. Growing old is a matter of *attitude*—not arteries.
2. Exercise your right to be happy.
3. Make your life meaningful and enjoyable.
4. To remain young, develop a gladness to be alive.
5. Forget the past. Live today. Make self-improvement a lifetime habit.
6. Examine your living habits. Avoid health dissipations.
7. Success is everything—but not without happiness.
8. Go after what you want in life, but after you get it, enjoy it.
9. Don't take yourself too seriously.
10. Live by the Golden Rule—treat your fellowman as you would want him to treat you.
11. Plan to be happy. The best things in life are planned.
12. Love of yourself and life is the best antidote to unhappiness.
13. Self-contentment is indispensable to happiness and enjoyment of life.
14. Loneliness is sugar-coated self-pity.
15. A positive self-image conquers loneliness.
16. Keep mentally active. It's anti-aging.
17. Positive thoughts during sessions of self-hypnotism can definitely help you enjoy better health.
18. Tell yourself morning and evening—"Every day I am improving in every way."
19. Grow wiser—not older.

20. Never stop learning.
21. Take pride in your appearance.
22. Gain self-confidence through accomplishments.
23. Take an inventory of yourself. Acknowledge your shortcomings and use the technique of self-hypnotism to correct them.
24. Develop a positive outlook on life which can be achieved via positive self-given suggestions.
25. Relax and enjoy.

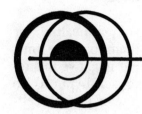

CHAPTER **12**

USING SELF-HYPNOSIS TO DEAL WITH BACKSLIDING

REALISM VERSUS NEGATIVISM

Backsliding is the resumption of unhealthy or unwanted habits after one has overcome them for some time.

The reader may infer that I am being negative in suggesting the possibility of anyone using self-hypnosis to backslide—that it is contradictory to the use of positive self-hypnotic suggestions.

However, there is a difference between negativism and realism. For example, it is not uncommon for anyone to resume the habit of smoking, drinking to excess or overeating, etc.

Despite good intentions, we are human, and capable of going back to unhealthy habits. But that doesn't mean we have to become discouraged and give up on ourselves. We have to remind ourselves that we can make a comeback, that we can refuse to be defeated.

Abraham Lincoln said it is better to make resolutions, even if we break them occasionally, than not to make them at all.

To be happy you have to work at being happy despite complications that tend to make you unhappy. Reality teaches you that life is a continual struggle for survival. But you can survive and still be a winner—you can make your life productive and enjoyable.

Habit control can be successful with self-hypnosis as pointed out in a previous chapter. Backsliding can be conquered with self-hypnosis. It takes stick-to-it-iveness, determination, and restoring your self-confidence. Perseverance is also necessary for resolving backsliding.

REINFORCED SESSIONS OF SELF-HYPNOSIS

Self-hypnosis can make the conquest of backsliding permanent. Here are some self-hypnotic suggestions to give yourself;

174

* I refuse to be a loser and return to an old unhealthy habit that proved detrimental to my physical and mental well-being.
* I am going to develop the ability to use my intellect to rule over my emotions to conquer whatever hangup I have.
* I am going to remind myself that I am in total control of my life.
* I will seek professional help and guidance if I need it.
* I am going to tell myself that successful self-management of my living habits is the key to self-contentment.
* I will never diminish my faith in self-hypnosis—that I can accomplish anything I make up my mind to accomplish.
* I am not going to think and act contrary to my well-being.
* I am going to apply what I have learned about self-hypnosis to overcome backsliding.
* I am going to develop emotional maturity—and not give way to habits that are self-destructive.
* I am going to remind myself that my future is going to depend on the way I think about myself.
* I will convince myself that a positive image of myself is the remedy for backsliding.
* I will use as many reinforced sessions of self-hypnosis as I need to ultimately overcome the resumption of unhealthy habits.
* I have the confidence that I can conquer backsliding—what my mind causes my same mind can cure.
* For every step backward I shall take two steps forward.

APPENDIX:

THE ROOTS OF HYPNOSIS

(In collaboration with Dr. Garland Fross,
President Emeritus, Association for the
Advancement of Ethical Hypnosis)

Understanding the history of hypnosis is indispensable to a better appreciation of why hypnosis has survived thousands of years up to our present time.

According to Dr. Garland Fross, in his *History of Hypnosis*, healing of their sick was believed to have been the power of saints, priests and medicine men, who found that if they attributed their power to their god or gods, they were revered and respected.

The Egyptians used hypnosis as therapy, referring to their places of self-therapy as "Sleep Temples."

Healing of the sick was carried out by means of prayers, ceremonies, laying on of the hands, drums, relics, and images. Moses was directed by the Lord to transmit his power and honor to Joshua by the laying of the hands.

The priests of the most ancient races, particularly in the Orient, were familiar with hypnosis. It was described in some of the earliest writings of India, Persia, Mongolia, Tibet, and China.

Dr. Bryan in his book *Religious Aspects of Hypnosis*, advances the theory that Jesus healed by hypnosis.

Among the ancient Greeks and Romans, Aesculapian healers often threw their patients into deep sleep and allayed pain by stroking with the hands.

Hippocrates, Father of Medicine said, "The affections suffered with the body, the soul sees quite well with shut eyes."

In the eleventh century Avicenna, a great physician of his day, wrote "Imagination of man could fascinate and modify a man's body, either making him ill or restoring him to health."

There was no name given for the phenomenon we now call hypnosis, nor was there any scientific explanation for it until Dr. Franz Anton Mesmer came along. Dr. Mesmer was a graduate of the Vienna Medical School in 1765.

While a student in medical school he observed several faith cures by a Catholic priest known as Father Gossner, who lived in Klosters, Austria. Mesmer refused to accept the theological, supernatural explanations of the phenomenon he saw. He sought a materialistic explanation. In those days, most illnesses and diseases were attributed to possession by demons. In this, Mesmer took no stock. He advanced the theory that the human body acts as a magnet with two poles, with an invisible magnetic fluid passing through the body and being thrown off at one end. Disease, then, to Mesmer, was an improper flow of fluid. The term mesmerism is still used today. It applies to passes made up and down over the body, without actual contact being made with the body. This was Mesmer's method of magnetizing the body.

Many remarkable cures of various types of illness were accomplished by Mesmer. What we now call psychosomatic illnesses were successfully cured. His fame grew in the five years he practiced in Vienna but because some of his demonstrations before hostile members of the medical profession failed, he was discredited, and so he moved to Paris. At that time, the method was surrounded by doubt and was easily discredited by a single failure.

For a while, Mesmer became famous in Paris. People flocked to him from all over France. He built a circular bath tub large enough to accommodate from eight to thirty people. On the floor of the tub were iron filings which had been magnetized. Over the filings were layers of bottles, with their necks converging toward a central point. The top was boarded up and iron rods from the center extended. Patients held on to the rods to receive the magnetic flow. This was Mesmer's famous "banquet."

The tub was in a darkened room in Mesmer's home. During the séance, there was orchestral music. At an appropriate moment Mesmer would enter, dressed in a silk robe and wearing a high conical hat. It was very theatrical. He would make passes over the patients who would go into convulsions. Each patient saw what happened to the others and was thereby conditioned to know what was expected of him. Mesmer thought the convulsions were the curative factor.

It was said by his enemies that Mesmer became obsessed

with the accumulation of wealth and glory. At any rate, in 1784 King Louis XVI appointed a commission of the scientists of the day to investigate him. This investigation was made on behalf of the Academy of Science. Our own Benjamin Franklin, at that time Ambassador to France, was a member of the commission. The trials and hearings ended the career of Mesmer, and he went into retirement in Switzerland. Franklin, however, in a minority report stated that there was something here which warranted future investigation, mentioning "imagination" as a possible factor. Franklin was ignored, and "animal magnetism" as it was called, was soon abandoned by all except a handful of followers. It was nearly a hundred years after Mesmer invented his technique that modern hypnosis came into its own.

After Mesmer's death, mesmerism was kept alive in France by his disciples.

In 1837, Oudet of France was the first dentist to extract a tooth painlessly by using suggestion anesthesia.

In 1842, Dr. James Braid, a Scotsman practicing medicine in Manchester, England, established the fact that *suggestion* is the dynamic force of hypnosis. This is the view accepted by practically all authorities today. Dr. Braid used hypnotic anesthesia for surgery. There was no chemical anesthesia in use at that time. Patients undergoing surgery were usually tied down or held down by a half-dozen strong arms, or whiskey was used to drug the patient into a drunken stupor. Although the medical profession looked on with hostility and suspicion, many physicians quietly used hypnosis as an anesthetic because there was nothing else to use.

The first use was in America. Hypnosis was used as a surgical anesthetic by Dr. Albert Wheeler when he cut a polyp from the nose of a patient. Dr. Phineas Quimby served as the anesthetist. Quimby was the stage hypnotist from whom Mary Baker Eddy got her idea for Christian Science.

In 1817, Dr. John Elliotson, Professor of Medicine at London University and President of the Royal Medical and Surgical Society, who, incidentally, introduced the stethoscope into England, proved the value of hypnosis in the treatment of nervous disorders as well as certain medical cases.

Dr. Liebault, a French country doctor in the mid-nineteenth century, referred to ten thousand cases treated successfully by hypnosis. Dr. Charcot was considered the greatest neurologist of his day and had his own clinic in Paris. He attempted to put hypnosis on a scientific basis in the last quarter of the nineteenth century.

Charcot was followed by Sigmund Freud who used hypnosis to probe the subconscious. Freud had the mistaken notion that a deep trance was necessary for therapeutic purposes. The patient was encouraged to talk under hypnosis and uncover lost memories of painful events of his past life. Freud ultimately abandoned the use of hypnosis and settled for psychoanalysis as his referred method of therapy.

Regarding the present status of hypnosis, it received the official sanction of the American Medical Association in 1958. After a two-year study of the A.M.A. Council on Mental Health it was found that "hypnosis has a recognized place in the medical armamentarium and is a useful technique when employed by qualified medical and dental personnel."

Dr. William Bryan re-introduced hypnosis to the Faculty of Medicine of France on September 11, 1958. It was the first time the subject had been presented to that medical body for one hundred and eighteen years.

At the present time there are four groups of scientific bodies using hypnosis. The first group is made up of the educational psychologists who use hypnosis to probe the mind, to study the mental processes and emotions. The second group is made up of the therapists who use hypnosis in the treatment of psychological disturbances. In the third group are those who use hypnosis primarily for relaxation, the elimination and control of pain. To this group belong the obstetricians and dentists. The fourth group are the hypno-technicians—lay hypnotists skilled in the induction and preparation of patients. They work closely with, and under the supervision of, the members of the dental and medical professions.

The Association to Advance Ethical Hypnosis, the hypno-technicians' parent organization, already numbers approximately fifteen hundred members and has chapters in twenty-four states. It appears that the hypno-technician, a specialist in his own right, and a valuable assistant when his services are indicated, is here today.

Hypnosis is a rapidly growing specialty. In 1958 there were no more than two hundred dentists and physicians in the United States using hypnosis. There is at the present time a minimum of 15,000 dentists and physicians using hypnosis.

Most of the instruction in hypnosis is now being given by teams of traveling dentists and physicians who offer three-and four-day and one-week post-graduate courses in dental and medical hypnosis. These courses are open to practicing dentists and physicians and persons in related fields.

I believe that the use of hypnosis should not be limited to physicans and dentists. It is a proven fact that many qualified and ethical hypno-technicians are capable of achieving successful therapeutic results.

Lectures regarding hypnosis and self-hypnosis should be made available to the general public. The inestimable value of self-hypnosis should inspire everyone to apply self-hypnosis to day-to-day self-improvement.

Hypnosis and self-hypnosis are gaining increasing importance in the lives of all human beings. The potentials are unlimited. I predict hypnosis will become a great force for the prevention of wars. War is a form of *insanity,* caused by *hate sickness,* irrational fears, uncontrolled aggressiveness, and unresolved conflicts arising from religious and other differences which account for the widespread violence we are presently witnessing. Hypnosis is based on the control of man's intellect over his emotions. Man's greatest triumph some day will be the conquest of himself so that he may teach others *it is better to love than to hate.*

It was J.B.S. Haldane, British scientist, who substantiated this when he stated:

"Anyone who has seen even a single example of the power of hypnosis and suggestion must realize that the face of the world and the possibilities of existence will be totally altered when we control their effects and standardize their application."

INDEX